CROSSING BETWEEN WORLDS

CROSSING BETWEEN WORLDS

The Navajo of Canyon de Chelly

Jeanne Simonelli
Wake Forest University

with Lupita McClanahan

PHOTOGRAPHS BY CHARLES WINTERS

WAVELAND

PRESS, INC.

Long Grove, Illinois

For information about this book, contact:
Waveland Press, Inc.
4180 IL Route 83, Suite 101
Long Grove, IL 60047-9580
(847) 634-0081
info@waveland.com
www.waveland.com

Frontispiece: Looking out toward hogan at Junction Farm.
All photographs by Charles Winters. Additional photographs on pages 113, 117, and 118 by Donatella Davanzo.

10-digit ISBN 1-57766-547-3
13-digit ISBN 978-1-57766-547-2

Printed in the United States of America

7   6   5   4   3   2   1

To the people of Canyon de Chelly
and to the Diné

Contents

JEANNE SIMONELLI is an anthropologist and writer who is professor of anthropology at Wake Forest University. Her field experiences are united by the broad theme of change and choice in difficult situations. She continues to work in the area of community development in Chiapas, Mexico, and is currently exploring the manipulation of social welfare policy by opposing forces in conflict situations. She received the 2000 prize for poetry from the Society for Humanistic Anthropology, and publishes both poetry and short stories based on field experiences. Her principal publications include *Uprising of Hope: Sharing the Zapatista Journey to Alternative Development* (2005) and *Two Boys, a Girl, and Enough!* (1986). In addition to *Crossing Between Worlds*, she has worked with Charles Winters on *Too Wet To Plow: The Family Farm in Transition* (1992).

CHARLES WINTERS is a photographer and cinematographer who teaches photography and digital photography at the State University in Oneonta, New York. His work has been widely exhibited and appears in a broad range of books.

Jeanne Simonelli and Charles Winters are currently working with Lupita McClanahan on a children's book for, and about, the Diné people.

Acknowledgments

It has been eighteen years since Charlie Winters and I first arrived in Arizona to try to record a period of change for the Navajos (*Diné*) who live and work in Canyon de Chelly. The experience resulted in lasting friendships and warm associations with many individuals. There is no way to adequately thank all those who participated for their cooperation and support over the years. Lupita Litson McClanahan; her husband, Jon; her daughter, Chris; and her mother, Susie, opened their homes and lives to us, as did Sara, Lena, Irene, and the other members of the family. Our hikes with Geno Bahe were always memorable, as was my time spent working with him in 1990 and 1991. The staff and administrators of Canyon de Chelly Nation Monument, including past superintendent Herbert Yahze and chief of interpretation Wilson Hunter, made it possible for us to be in the canyon as volunteers and guests. Many others are not thanked here by name, but their kindness has always been valued. We hope that they will see themselves portrayed in these pages with the dignity and strength that were evident to us throughout the years. All the canyon residents who so generously shared their lives with us are given pseudonyms in the text that follows.

In addition to moral support, this project could not have proceeded without material and professional backing. Grants from the SUNY-Oneonta Development Council and the United University Professions provided partial funding. The Tamron Corporation furnished some of the lenses used in this project. Technical support was provided by the State University College at Oneonta, especially the staff of the Instructional Resources Center. The SAR Press staff provided help and encouragement throughout the editorial and publication process for the original edition: past directors Joan O'Donnell and Jane Kepp supported the project and went out of their way to see it to completion; Jo Ann Baldinger was a sensitive and skilled editor of the first edition text; and Deborah Flynn Post showed insight and care in designing the book. Other commentaries were provided by Lupita Litson, Patricia Honan-Wohlford, Stephen Trimble, and three anonymous reviewers.

At Waveland Press, Tom Curtin's support for this updated second edition was critical. The ability to keep this book in print allows us to keep faith with our promise to all those canyon residents and their families who opened their lives to us. This edition also includes photos by anthropologist Donatella Davanzo, who stayed with Margarita's family in 2007. These capture the ways we have all changed since the initial period depicted in these pages. As can be seen, change has happened faster for the children, and this work is for them.

The completion of a creative work is not always a smooth process. Consequently, a debt of gratitude is owed to our families. Charlie's wife, Martha Leigh, was an avid supporter throughout this project and a willing participant during a month of camping without showers at Canyon de Chelly. Charlie's daughter, Natasha, was, as always, enthusiastic about the photographic imagery. My daughter, Elanor, gave me food for thought during my first summer at the canyon. My daughter, Rachel, grew from child to woman during this work, and her support at home made it possible for me to travel and write. Though Rachel never revisited the canyon after the summer of 1990, she remained an important intersection in the unfolding story, since "Margarita" and I were both mothers of teenage girls and faced similar dilemmas.

Finally, I still thank my beloved dog and companion, Josafin, who took me on daily walks during the original writing of this book, providing an opportunity to think and work out the details. I know she would have typed the manuscript if she had been able to. As with so many of those who started this journey in 1990, she has passed over into another world. This edition especially commemorates each of their lives.

Foreword to the Second Edition

Dictated by Grandma Karen to her daughter, Margarita, July 25, 2007

I've learned to open the pages to *Crossing Between Worlds* book without help now. When I look at the pictures, it brings me *ho zho'*—beauty. It helps me make my past clear; the book is one of the best things that ever happened. Especially for today, it seems like all our children only understand the books. When we talk Diné it's hard for them to understand. But, I enjoy it when they teach me about the story books; I especially like my book, *Crossing Between Worlds*.

The *yei' bi' cheii'* farmland in the canyon is better to see now. I feel my grandmothers and their grandmothers are happy; it brings joy to my heart. I am very thankful for my daughter Pete and my son [in-law] Jon who work and improve the yei' bi cheii canyon farm. Our clan *kinya' aah nii* has more land at Junction area, but I don't know why my sister's children and my children don't work with the land anymore. They probably don't have time for it anymore. Me, I can't haul water anymore and I can't chop wood anymore. My eyes have been playing tricks on me.

I wish I still had my young eyes. Modern world Doctor said they can put an animal eye or someone that died in my eye so I can see better, but I totally disagree. I'm going to have nightmares every night and I'm not going to sleep and then my eyes will always be closed and that is what I don't want. Modern Doctors are sometimes goofy. But we love our friend Dr. Tori from Portland; she is a naturopathic Doctor. She loves to learn more about the plants and how we cure ourselves with our plants. My life

Grandma Karen prepares bread at her home at Black Rock on the peninsula.

in the canyon has been limited but my heart is always there for the land. About six years ago my clan uncle said, "My legs are hanging over the death world, it won't be long before it arrives for me." There's some things my elders said that I won't forget.

Nature seems to be different, too; it doesn't feel the same way like it used to be twenty years ago or so. The cold weather is longer and warm weather is shorter and the weather seems to be hazier all the time. People don't cook; they always eat Basha's food. It's a little bit scary. But my future is my grandchildren. I love them dearly.

My heart is always with my home, Black Rock, DezAh, and Canyon de Chelly. My children tell me that I'll get lost in the snow at night if I go outside for the outhouse at Black Rock. Black Rock recently got electricity but we still don't have running water for plumbing. People are still not used to having electricity. And we still have twenty miles of dirt road and it gets impossible to travel on especially in the winter. In the meantime my children put me in a modern house at Tsaile Solar Housing which is closer to the clinic.

My children that live in the east, Charlie and Jeanne, probably have grandchildren now; I wish I could see them. I can just imagine that they have beautiful green eyes and beautiful shiny hair. I just wonder how many grandchildren they have now. Maybe some day they will come and speak to me. I also love their children. I remember my daughter Pete telling me that we have a New York fence—fence that Jeanne and her daughter made in the canyons. The canyon and the wonderful book *Crossing Between Worlds* brought us many wonderful friends from all over the world; my heart goes out to all of them and their loved ones. Now, all my people, especially my great grandfather, will be happy because we now have lots of relatives.

CANYON DE CHELLY

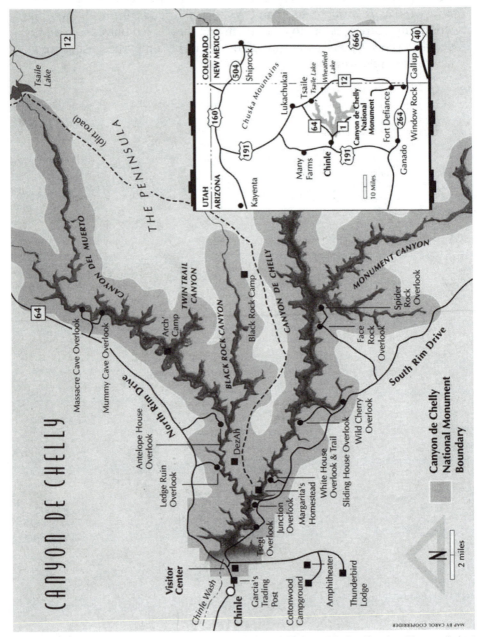

Finding the Trail

This story began with my daughter, who loved horses as only a young girl could, and with my own passion for mesas. Rachel and I lived in a small community in rural New York, a place of sweet, gentle, green hills where brief summer is followed by endless November. In the winter of 1990 the gray was particularly damp and dense, the snow forgot to fall, and the deep turquoise skies of Arizona and New Mexico drifted in and out of my waking dreams.

An anthropologist by trade, I had been teaching at the State University of New York at Oneonta for five years and also led biannual "on-the-road" summer programs in the Southwest. These five-week rambles took my students and me to national parks and monuments where we followed rangers through ruins and canyons and up and down the hand- and toe-hold trails. I always admired our well-versed tour guides. Now, as the winter wore on, I decided to realize a childhood dream. I applied for a job as a seasonal park ranger.

I filled out the lengthy National Park Service application in December, designating two park sites for potential employment. My choices were based on two considerations. I'm happiest in the dry heat and piñon-juniper woodlands of the Southwest, so the park had to be in that part of the country. Even more important, it had to be a place where eleven-year-old Rachel could spend the entire day in the company of horses. I picked Mesa Verde, Colorado, because it was close to a large tourist town I assumed would have horses, and Canyon de Chelly, Arizona, because of the riding stable located at the mouth of the canyon.

In April, with spring semester drawing to a close, a woman from the interpretive branch at Mesa Verde called to offer me a seasonal position. "I have a preteen daughter," I told her. "I'm sorry," she answered. "We can't have children here. Housing, you know." I wondered if my career as a park ranger was doomed before it began.

Three days later, a wet spring snow was falling when the phone rang. This time it was the chief of interpretation at Canyon de Chelly National Monument. Visions of sunlight and warmth filled my head as he described the job. I was needed as a seasonal ranger by May 10; the position lasted through Labor Day; they would pay me to hike and talk and do the things I normally did for recreation. Anticipating another rejection, I told him I had a child.

"Great!" he replied. "We'll put another bed in the duplex. This is a Navajo park. One of the other seasonals has a baby. We're family." So, right from the start, I had the feeling that Canyon de Chelly would be a special place.

As a single parent and homeowner, I faced some immediate logistical dilemmas. What about the house? Who would care for our loving but neurotic dog? What should we tell Rachel's elementary school, where the term continued until the end of June? Luckily, obstacles are easily overcome when a dream calls to us. By early May, Rachel and I were ready to go, our lives packed into two large suitcases and a cardboard box. Less than twenty-four hours after I turned in my final grades, we flew from New York to Albuquerque.

Two Navajo rangers were waiting at the airport to drive us to Canyon de Chelly, just outside Chinle, Arizona, and four hours from Albuquerque. The approach to the canyon is not encouraging. Chinle is a dismal cluster of convenience stores, fast-food franchises, coin laundries, and video rental establishments. Its low complex of schools is surrounded by a chain-link fence cluttered with hand-lettered signs announcing community activities. Farther down the road, a red-striped chicken bucket offsets the hexagonal shape of the Catholic Church. To either side, the pale, fragile-looking layers of Chinle sandstone look more like the unkempt remains of strip mining than a natural formation.

I began to feel apprehensive as we drew near the entrance to the monument. My previous visits to Canyon de Chelly had been as a tourist. I had focused on its spectacular beauty and archaeological significance, ignoring the realities of the daily life of the Navajo people whose home this was. Now, looking through a new lens, I saw open-range cattle rummaging through sparse vegetation at the side of the road and government-built housing falling into disrepair in the dry dust.

During the drive from Albuquerque, the soft-spoken Navajo rangers told us about the upcoming three-day training hike and orientation for new staff. We would be joined by Navajo and non-Navajo naturalists, healers, archaeologists, and others with special knowledge of the canyon. The rangers assured me that Rachel was welcome; in fact, other kids would meet us as we hiked a twenty-mile stretch of the north side of the canyon.

On the training hike I met the people I would be working with for the next four months. Together we would staff the visitor center, hike the trails, and present programs. Our workday was ten hours long, but I seldom looked at a clock. Some days I was up and out by 7:30 AM, dressed in baseball cap, short-sleeved shirt, and hiking shorts, ready to lead the morning hike. On other days I was in the amphitheater at 9 PM in full dress uniform, welcoming visitors to Canyon de Chelly with a multimedia evening program. Rachel, meanwhile, apprenticed herself to the local riding stable. On her own mount she accompanied her Navajo coworkers as they guided visitors through the wash while I held forth to a trailing group of morning hikers. I was learning. I was looking.

The Park Service, like the tourists, is in the canyon as a guest of the Navajo people. Canyon de Chelly has been home to the Navajos since the early 1700s and remains both a place of residence and a location of great sacred significance. Meanwhile, the number of visitors to the area has been increasing steadily as the canyon's fame spreads worldwide. The legislation establishing Canyon de Chelly as a national monument in 1931 gave the National Park Service primary responsibility for the management of prehistoric resources and tourism in order to "preserve its prehistoric ruins and features of scientific or historical interest." During the time I worked there, it became evident that the current goals were broader and more complex than simple preservation. Visitors are still encouraged to experience the canyon's scenic and archaeological beauty, but they are also reminded they are on Navajo land and must respect the privacy of the residents. Moreover, tourism must take place in a way that does not cause further deterioration of the archaeological resources.

The Navajo Nation retains ownership of the land within the park, thus necessitating a relationship with the Park Service that requires constant, and not always easy, communication. Though the monument provides employment for local residents, many Navajos suspect the federal government's intentions. The long-standing (and historically well-founded) fear that the government will eventually force residents to leave their homes, fields, and flocks resurfaces constantly. Few Navajos were involved in the decision to designate the canyon as a protected area in 1931. Today, tribal members are closer to policy decisions than in the past, but after renewed discussion in the 1990s, responsibility for management still rests with the National Park Service.

I came to Canyon de Chelly to be a ranger, not an anthropologist. More than half of my coworkers were Navajos from the canyon, skilled in translating their culture for the benefit of visitors. The remainder of the staff was non-Navajos and included professionals trained in some branch of anthropology or natural history, as well as volunteers with educational

backgrounds and interests that coincided with the monument's needs. Working side by side, we engaged in a continuous exchange of values and perceptions.

As I walked through the deep, saffron-hued corridors of the canyon, I pondered the remains left by prehistoric dwellers and exchanged shy greetings with grandmothers clad in long velvet skirts. The anthropologist in me was fascinated by the struggle of my Navajo friends to create a balance between the two cultures. Questions began to form in my mind. Could the volume of tourism be increased without altering the age-old cultural terrain? Could the Navajos continue to use the canyon's resources to meet their physical and spiritual needs without altering the natural and archaeological landscape? Could the Park Service preserve and conserve the fragile archaeological resources of the canyon while also encouraging tourism? How did the Navajos view the process of change, and to what extent did they want to share in the values and material goods being brought into the area from the non-Navajo world?

Even as I thought about these practical questions, I was experiencing Canyon de Chelly in a new and deeply personal way. I watched the flickering tongues of a bonfire send dancing shadows against the canyon wall during the training hike. Later, I listened to stories of creation and continuity, learning about the Navajo Way. I found myself asking questions that had long been silenced by my quest for security and material comfort, by work and school and parenting, by VCRs and automobiles. Now, as I hiked side canyons and scrambled up talus slopes, more profound issues began to surface. How did my beliefs and values contribute to a world on the verge of ecological crisis? How had I ignored the interconnectedness between living things that was so basic to the worldview of my Navajo coworkers? How could I achieve a sense of harmony with the universe?

I was sometimes disappointed, that first summer, by how long it took to develop friendships with the other rangers. In fact, Rachel was learning more about Navajo culture than I was. Adopted into the family of her "employers," she spent much of her time in their home and picked up some of the Navajo language. Near the end of the season, however, I was invited to spend some days in the canyon with one of my Navajo coworkers and her family. I had worked with Margarita Dawson for almost four months, listening to her musical voice describe Navajo traditions to fascinated visitors. Now, with Labor Day approaching, she and I were the only two seasonal employees left, and we started talking to each other in the quiet times between our official duties.

One evening at the end of our shift, Margarita suggested that we hike to the floor of the canyon along White House Trail. Her sister had a tradi-

Previous page: Canyon horse near White House Ruins.

tional hogan near the junction of Canyon de Chelly and Canyon del Muerto, the two main branches of the park. We rangers hiked that trail at least three times a week; it was so familiar that I would have sworn I could hike it in my sleep.

The August night was chilly and new-moon black. We started down the trail, stepping cautiously. After ten minutes we paused, measuring the faint, starlit shadows against the slope of the path. Margarita's voice floated across to me through the darkness.

"Where's the trail?" she called out in disbelief. We stumbled into each other, laughing and shuddering as we pictured the sheer, six-hundred-foot drop below us. We picked our way carefully in search of the dried mud switchbacks.

Down below a horse whinnied. The sound echoed against the sandstone, startling us. "It's that white horse," Margarita said. "That horse has been down there close to fifteen years. He's wild. Nobody can catch him."

I easily pictured the white horse, a constant observer of my morning hikes. My pack and sleeping bag bounced against my back as I bent over, hoping to find a line of marking stone amid the low grass and gravel. Suddenly Margarita turned. There was the trail, exactly where it should have been, a little to the left and just beyond a line of swaying greasewood.

Relieved, we stood in the night and talked about our lives and our dreams. Like the trail, the road to our friendship lay clear before us. We began walking it together that evening, setting out on what was to be a journey of questions and discovery for each of us, our families, and our friends.

One friend of mine who would come to know Margarita and her family was photographer Charles Winters, whom I met when I first began teaching at SUNY. Charlie was the campus photographer and had already completed a book about the rural counties surrounding the college. Discovering a mutual admiration for Lewis Hines and the photographic social documentary tradition of the 1930s, we decided to collaborate on a book. The result was *Too Wet to Plow* (New Amsterdam Press, 1990), which documented the decline of the family farm in upstate New York. A story of social and cultural change, using ethnography and photography as investigative tools, it was designed for the general public as well as the anthropological community.

The success of that project led me to contemplate a similar work about the families of Canyon de Chelly. I was interested in exploring the changes occurring in the lives of canyon families, as well as the complex set of relationships between the Navajo people, the Park Service, and the canyon visitors. Before leaving the canyon in September of 1990, I showed Margarita a copy of *Too Wet to Plow* and asked how she would feel about a book that focused on her family and the families of other Navajo rangers.

Margarita passed the book around to members of her family, as she would do later with the photographs and text of the original edition of this book. To my surprise, she invited Charlie and me to return in the winter to visit and photograph at a time when the winter tales could be told. I accepted and, in anticipation, presented a proposal for the work to the Park Service. I needed their approval in order to be in the canyon. After much discussion, it was agreed that Charlie and I would provide volunteer services in exchange for canyon access.

This book has its roots in the experience of that first summer. It was nurtured by the cooperation and patience of many Navajo people who would eventually become friends. Over the next five years Charlie and I returned frequently to Canyon de Chelly—sometimes together, sometimes separately. At times these visits were exhilarating; at times they were painful reminders that understanding and friendship bloom only as the products of time, good intentions, conversation, and contemplation. Much of what we learned from one another has helped us in our common attempt to create a balance between the logic of tradition and the relentless demands of the twenty-first century. It is my hope that this book will stand as testimony to the lives of the people of Canyon de Chelly and to the continuing growth of respect and appreciation between our cultures.

Chapter 1

Facing East

"Did you bring this weather with you from New York, Jeanne?" asked Margarita Dawson with a smile, referring to the cold, thick cloud that surrounded the Canyon de Chelly Visitor Center. "Good to see you," she added.

I laughed. "Wouldn't be the first time East Coast weather followed me." I walked forward and we exchanged a light handshake. Margarita's gaze fell on the bearded man standing beside the rental car parked outside the visitor center. "I want you to meet my good friend Charlie," I said, emphasizing "friend" in response to the question in Margarita's eyes.

Charlie Winters and I had flown into Phoenix in mid-January of 1991 on our first visit to Arizona together. The sky was clear as we drove across the Navajo Reservation, but when we turned north at Ganado a dense, frozen fog hung in a wide circle around Canyon de Chelly. It grew thicker as we moved toward Park Service headquarters and seemed to reflect my apprehension about coming here with Charlie and his cameras to do fieldwork. The start of a new project invariably brought up my concerns about the nature and complexity of anthropological research. Did I still have the skill to tell someone else's story with accuracy and sensitivity?

We arranged to stay in the same duplex where I lived the previous summer as a ranger. In exchange for the housing, I would help out in the visitor center and Charlie would photograph rock art for the monument's interpretive collection. Aside from these commitments, we planned to spend as much time as possible with Margarita and her large family.

Margarita walked forward and extended her hand to Charlie. "*Yá'át'ééh*. Welcome to Canyon de Chelly. I'll get the key to the housing and let you in to get settled. There's a ceremony tonight, and I can't stay long right now. But I can meet you in the canyon tomorrow if you'd like, and Thursday some of my relatives are coming down. You can help us fix the Park Service hogan. Mix the mud. Chink the walls. Keep you working."

I laughed again. Fieldwork was a constant dichotomy. Either you were busy twenty hours of the day, or there was nothing happening. Charlie and I had come to the canyon in winter to learn the stories and games that took place only in the long months "when thunder sleeps." During the summer my Navajo friends had alluded to these stories and especially to *késhjéé'*, the shoe game, a traditional bout of chance and choice. Thanks in large part to Margarita's determination to reintroduce traditions that had begun to fade as change moved through the reservation, a shoe game was set for Friday night.

A chill blast of wind rustled the crystal-covered fronds of a large yucca in front of the visitor center as we waited for Margarita to bring the keys. Winter had been bitter and brutal at Canyon de Chelly that year. December temperatures dropped to fourteen below, colder than most people could remember. On the peninsula that divided the monument into two deep canyons, the family "elderlies" weathered the frigid days, splitting brittle juniper to warm the *hooghans* with fragrant cedar fires. Inside each of these traditional homes, called "hogan" in English, a barrel stove sizzled. Goats and sheep huddled together in the corrals, crying out against the piercing wind that penetrated their winter wool.

The New Year brought snow as deep as a standing lamb, covering the ochre-and-orange canyon rims and laying a thick coat across the gray, frozen twists of the Chinle Wash. The frozen wash was a good sign, for it had been close to dry the previous winter, and most of the summer as well. The snow cover promised even more water in the spring, abundant moisture for the April planting of corn and alfalfa on the canyon floor.

Charlie and I settled into the duplex and Margarita headed next door where she was spending the winter with her aged and ailing father. She had a house twenty-five miles east at Tsaile but wanted to be with her father near the Chinle hospital complex. Her preteen daughter, Carla, remained with family in Tsaile in order to attend school, and Margarita commuted back and forth between her responsibilities.

The canyon was still blanketed in fog the next morning when Charlie and I drove up the south rim to the White House Ruin overlook. The fog hung like a swaying mass from Wild Cherry Canyon to Ganado, west to Many Farms, and east to Nazlini. An occasional light wind moved the cloud like disturbed bathwater, first one way and then another. At such moments, the fog broke slightly and there was sunlight, incredibly blue sky, and a touch of warmth.

Locking the car, Charlie grabbed his cameras and we started down the stiff mud switchbacks of the White House Trail. Across from White House Ruin a group of visitors contemplated braving the chill waters of the wash to get closer to the fenced-in structure. The hardier ones removed their socks and boots, rolled up their pants, and waded across. I walked gingerly through an area that was quicksand in the warmer months and broke through the crust, sinking into the mud. My cry of distress startled an old Navajo woman who stood across the wash, surrounded by small collie-like dogs. A flock of sheep and goats rooted around for food in the dried sage and rabbitbrush. The woman looked at me and pointed to a larger dog.

"Mother," she said simply.

I walked to her and tried a few Navajo words. " *Tl'izí*—goat; *ts'ah*—sagebrush; *zas* snow." She didn't seem to understand, which was no surprise. I knew a few nouns but couldn't link them together, and my pronunciation was that of any inexperienced *biligáana*—white person. A wave of anxiety and helplessness swept over me. How could I do my part of this work if I didn't speak the language? Would it be possible to know the older Navajos through a translator, to understand anything about their lives and their relationship to the land and people around them? What were Charlie and I *doing* here?

Fording the wash, we continued walking through the canyon. Two horses grazed behind a fence, woolly coated with the thick fur of winter. I thought of my daughter, Rachel, who had remained in New York to take care of her horse, Snip. These canyon horses were on their own; no starry-eyed teenaged girl would bring them hay or sweet feed to see them through the cold months. Then I noticed some green grass growing in a sheltered corner of a side canyon. The horses would do all right.

Charlie and I spent the morning hiking and photographing rock art. Then we went to meet Margarita on the land she and her sisters had been given by their mother, a part of the old family farm near the junction of the two canyons. Margarita hoped to reestablish a working farm at the place where she had lived as a child. Beginning slowly, she had already built a shade house, a shelter, and a cooking area.

As with most canyon locales, the whole area's history and prehistory could be found in the rock art, structures, and artifacts. "It's still here," Margarita explained, "because Navajo teaching told us to stay away from the places of the ancient ones, to leave their arrowheads and pottery and buildings alone." She equated Navajo traditional prohibitions about entering ruins with the Park Service edict to "preserve and protect."

The previous summer Margarita seemed the most conservative of all my Navajo coworkers. On our first training hike she lingered behind the rest of us to say appropriate prayers while a visiting botanist cut plants for collection. When we worked together in the canyon, she always asked me to be the one to enter the ruins to check for signs of vandalism or destruction. But this year Margarita had begun to venture into archaeological sites herself, as part of her job and because of her growing interest in the story that the ruins could tell about the canyon.

Now, as Margarita built a fire to cook an early supper, her daughter Carla joined Charlie and me as we walked around the perimeter of the farm, close against the six-hundred-foot cliff wall. Because it had been such a dry year, vegetation was sparse. Erosion, that great archaeologist, had laid bare another level of earth, and the ground between the clumps of rabbitbrush was scattered with pottery and projectiles.

"Pick that up," said Carla matter-of-factly, pointing to a fine pink chert point lying at her feet. Without thinking, I obeyed, cradling the thousand-year-old point in the palm of my hand. Carla found a piece of dried greasewood and used it to poke and prod and turn the arrowhead as I held it. "Who made that?" she asked. "How old is it, do you think?" She could not touch the point, but that did not stop her from being curious about it. "I can touch the white ones," she explained, "because I'm a girl. If they are whole, I can keep them. But I can't touch anything else."

"What's the difference between whole white ones and broken pink ones?" I asked, looking for symbolism and meaning. Carla dropped the greasewood stick. "I don't know," she said. "I don't know if my mother knows either. You'll have to ask my grandma."

Other Navajos living in the canyon were less meticulous about following the teachings. "Used to play Tonka toys in there," one of the guides at the stable had told me the previous summer, as we paused together near a small site. "Knock down walls. Great fun!" "Wonderful place to play dolls," said a second as I listened, my Park Service persona horrified.

Carla, Charlie, and I continued walking past the bare apple and apricot trees to an area where the artifacts, structures, and rock art spanned fifteen hundred years. One panel of drawings pecked into the stone depicted a curious gathering of seated figures, each holding a staff of some kind. We agreed that the staffs looked like weavers' spindles—a reasonable conclusion, since the Anasazi wove fine cotton cloth more than eight hundred years ago. Farther down the cliff wall were drawings of deer and antelope in bright pigments. Charlie took out his cameras and began to photograph. Margarita joined us.

"What do you think they are? Why are they different?" she asked. She was referring to the two forms of rock art in Canyon de Chelly: petroglyphs and pictographs. Petroglyphs are pictures and symbols pecked into the rock with strong, sharpened implements, usually made of antler, bone, or stone. They are found on standing rocks and cliff faces, in areas where the desert varnish or patina has left a flat, darkened surface. In contrast, pictographs are images painted with protein-based pigments. The colors include white, yellow, blue-green, red, and black, and they correspond to calcium carbonate, yellow ochre, turquoise, red ochre or red sandstone, and charcoal, respectively. Mixed with a binder that included saliva, blood, egg, or urine, the crushed minerals formed incredibly durable paints. Brushes were made of yucca wands, frayed at the bottom to produce a fibrous tool. A favorite ranger pastime was to stop during the morning hike, crush pigment on a rock, add some spit, make a brush, and create an impromptu painting.

Some of my Navajo friends used the generic term "rockarts" to describe all of the visible design elements and styles. When we hiked in the canyon, they would explain the more contemporary works we came upon—cowboy boot petroglyphs that marked footpaths, incised horse hooves to indicate stock trails.

Like Margarita, I wondered what the prehistoric drawings signified. Did they represent art, graffiti, religious writings, or the communication of environmental information? Were they designed to convey a specific message in a particular location? Could we ever really do more than make informed guesses? Navajo tradition holds that the prehistoric pictures dated from the time and dimension when the Holy Ones walked among the Earth People. When they left, they put images onto rocks and into stone. Afterward, it became inappropriate for humans to make permanent markings on rocks.

"Want to climb up and look?" Carla asked, indicating a carved hand-and toe-hold trail heading up the side of the cliff to what seemed to me a precarious level. With rock art, accessibility of the location is not an issue—in fact, inaccessibility may have been a virtue. Carla was goading me; she knew I was not so much afraid of heights as of edges. She'd been raised from toddlerhood to climb using these trails, but I had grown up, like most biligáana, hearing my mother yell, "Don't climb up there!" The cliff was still coated with a light frost. I shook my head. "Next time. In the spring."

Supper was ready, and we started back toward the blazing juniper fire. I wondered if Margarita really wanted an answer from me about meaning and rock art, or if we were just comparing opinions. Sometimes when I found myself poised on the verge of an academic lecture in answer to a question, I had to stop myself. I was not here as a teacher. I had come here to learn. It would take a while for me to realize that in a culture based on reciprocity, knowledge, too, was an even exchange.

"Does it ever snow here?" summer visitors had often asked as they gazed along the heat-parched slopes of the canyon. Imagining a Southwest cloaked in snowfall is difficult for those passing through in July. For the Navajos, though, the long months of frigid winter are a time for learning and for recounting tales of the coming of the Diné—the People—to these lands.

It was in the winter months when families gathered around the hogan fire to hear grandfathers and uncles tell the stories of creation.

Navajo history is one of emergence, of the long journey of living creatures from the First World to the Fourth. Here, in this glittering Fourth
World between the four sacred mountains of the Navajo homeland, First
Man and First Woman were formed. Here they learned the skills needed
to survive as human beings in a land blessed each day by Sunbearer and
the other Holy People. In winter, then, you heard stories about Coyote,
the perennial trickster and bungler, and the Great Gambler at Chaco
Canyon to the east, and learned how the stone houses of the Anasazi, the
Ancient Ones, came to be.

"I like the winter!" said Noreen, Margarita's aunt, grabbing a handful
of mud and taking aim at the wall of the Park Service hogan. "In winter
you get to slow down."

It was mid afternoon and getting colder with each passing hour.
Snow threatened as Charlie and I joined Margarita and other family
members to help make repairs. The eight-sided hogan, built of long
lengths of ponderosa pine, had been closed to visitors for six years
because of a cracked beam. Margarita's wish to hold a shoe game there
had spurred the Park Service to authorize the repairs we were making.

I stood up from where I was tearing strips of juniper bark to use as
temper between the horizontal logs of the hogan and looked at Noreen.
She was a short, wiry, exuberant woman, not much older than Margarita
herself. Her wide grin enlivened her entire face.

"I like winter, too," I answered. "Except that once the snow begins to
fall, it's so hard to get to work, or pick Rachel up after school, or go gro-
cery shopping." Noreen scooped up some more mud and took aim again.
"But that's the point, Jeanne," she said with amusement. "Of course it's
difficult. You're not supposed to go anywhere when the winter comes.
You're just supposed to stay home." I looked at Charlie. "Be nice to live
in a place where the pace of life is supposed to parallel natural and biolog-
ical rhythms," he said. I nodded in agreement.

Noreen moved closer to the stove where Margarita, her sister Lora,
and her cousin Linda were mixing orange sand with warm water to make
the mortar. Lora fingered the sand thoughtfully and reminisced about eating dirt by the handful when she was a child in the canyon. "Why did we
do that?" she wondered aloud.

I watched the women bury four shoes in shallow rectangular pits in
the dirt floor on either side of the stove. Tonight, players would break up
into teams. One set of shoes was buried to the south, for the team called
"Day," and the other to the north, for the "Night" team. In each round of
the game one team would hide a little stone ball—*tólásht'óshí*—in one of
the shoes, which was then completely covered with dirt. The opposing

Previous page: Spider Rock during winter snow.

team would try to figure out where the ball was hidden. It is said that in the very first competition, the animals played to see which condition would prevail, darkness or light. That game resulted in a tie, and that is why there are both night and day.

When we returned to the hogan four hours later, a steady snow began to fall. The flakes drifted slowly through the smoke hole in the cribbed-log roof of the hogan, swirled in the yellow-orange glow of the single lantern, and came to rest on the heated surface of the metal stove, where they melted. The women set a table with cookies, coffee, and punch for participants to share between the long rounds of the game.

One hundred and two yucca leaves (*k'et'ááz*), to be used for keeping score, lay near the stove alongside a juniper wand used to select the correct shoe. Clustered on either side of a raised blanket, the two teams alternately hid the ball or planned strategies for choosing the correct shoe.

The players, representing the animals of the day and night, accumulated yucca for each correct choice, each team striving for the full count of 102. Since the match was just for fun, nobody was betting, but this in no way diminished the excitement as the game progressed, accompanied by bawdy songs and jokes in Navajo.

The evening's game was juxtaposed against a different kind of conflict. Far beyond the hogan and the reaches of the Navajo Nation, the Persian Gulf War was beginning. During a pause between rounds one of the older men called us into a circle to clasp hands and pray. The speaker talked quietly in Navajo, remembering the men of the community who had already gone to fight. As Margarita translated, I joined them in English, thinking of my older daughter, Elanor, whose Army Reserve unit would probably be called up. Together we asked that this inexplicable war not last, nor bring sadness and death to the canyon; we asked that, in this global game of chance, night would not win out over day.

Six inches of snow fell on the night of the shoe game, filling the spaces between blue-green juniper and piñon trees and covering the tall spines of the previous summer's yucca. In the early morning, children bundled in parkas and boots waited for the school bus. A half-foot of snow was not enough to close the schools, relieving bus drivers accustomed to covering more than a hundred miles each day on rutted reservation roads.

That morning, Charlie and I were joined by our friend Ben, a tall, sandy-haired youth with a strong resemblance to Earl H. Morris, an archaeologist who had worked in the canyon in the 1920s. Ben was Morris's grandson, and this was his first visit here since childhood. The Park Service gave me permission to take him to some of the places where his grandfather had excavated more than sixty years before.

The beginning of the twentieth century saw the emergence of the new field of archaeology and the beginning of extensive digging throughout the region known as the Four Corners, where Arizona, Utah, Colorado, and New Mexico meet. Canyon de Chelly was an exception because the early archaeologists believed there was nothing left to find there. Collectors and explorers had already been through, gathering multicolored ceramic vessels to sell in the East. One of these was Sam Day, who in 1902 established a trading post at the mouth of Canyon de Chelly, where the Thunderbird Lodge now sits. (The post was housed in the long log building that is now the lodge cafeteria.) When they were not trading supplies for crafts made by canyon residents, Day and his family roamed the area looting prehistoric sites for pots, baskets, and other artifacts.

In 1906, one of the famous (or infamous) Wetherill brothers carved his last name in the well-polished sandstone near the tower of Mummy Cave, the most magnificent of the canyon's ruins, then moved on. Though some journals and notes document the activities of adventurers like the Wetherills, the greater part of what they collected will never be known. As a result of this assumed plunder, formal expeditions to Canyon de Chelly were not mounted until 1923, when Earl Morris drove his Model T Ford through the deep sand of Canyon del Muerto to Mummy Cave. A year later, with the backing of the American Museum of Natural History, he began a series of explorations into the origins of the oldest of the Ancient Ones to leave their tale in the twin canyons.

Morris was most interested in the people whom the archaeologists called "Basketmakers," who occupied the Canyon de Chelly system from about AD 250 to 700. The Basketmaker people hunted in the area and gathered abundant wild plants including grasses, greens, and gourds. As they settled within the fertile canyon, they began cultivating corn, squash, and, later, beans. They built their houses of brush and poles, often at the back of alcoves high above the canyon floor. By about AD 500, walled and roofed shelters were being built as houses in shallow pits, and harvests were stored in slab-lined cysts, thus providing a food supply for the long winters. Domesticated turkeys became an added resource, valued for their feathers as well as their meat. The Basketmakers were accomplished weavers who made fine baskets, bags, sandals, and mats from the combined fibers of yucca and hemp, feathers and fur.

Toward the end of this period, the people living in the de Chelly area, like others throughout the Southwest, began building larger homes from less perishable materials. They hunted with the bow and arrow as well as the older atlatl, or spear-thrower. In addition, they lined their baskets with unfired clay, a preliminary to producing actual ceramic vessels, which were in widespread use throughout the Southwest by AD 500.

Mummy Cave as photographed from the North Rim.

As population in the Four Corners area grew between AD 700 and 1100, settlements became larger and more complex and featured large multi-roomed masonry dwellings. Cotton was added to the list of cultivated crops. In the farming communities of Canyon de Chelly and Canyon del Muerto, this period saw the building of kivas (underground chamber associated with both weaving and religious practice) and elaborate villages whose remnants include the ruins of Mummy Cave, White House, and Antelope House.

The people who built and occupied these communal villages, or pueblos, became known to twentieth-century excavators as the Anasazi, and more recently as the Ancestral Pueblos. The name Anasazi, used by Morris's colleague A. V. Kidder to describe the continuum of people who had occupied the northern Southwest, came from the Navajo word *anaasází*, or enemy ancestors. Kidder thought it simply meant "old people."

Between 1923 and 1932, Morris mounted extensive excavations in the area around Mummy Cave and Antelope House. At times he worked with Kidder, but most often he was accompanied by his wife, artist and writer Ann Axtell Morris. The journal she kept of their time in Canyon del Muerto became the source for her book *Digging in the Southwest*, a colorful and sensitive supplement to Morris's notes on the excavations. Camped at Mummy Cave in the 1920s, Ann Morris expressed the mystery of the place, a mystery still sensed by those who live in or visit the canyon. Speaking of the Basketmaker people, she wrote:

These ancient dwellings were quite different from the standard Cliff Houses which came to occupy the cave later, of which the elaborate masonry tower is an example. The old long-skulls were content with more primitive things. Their houses . . . were single rooms, roughly circular in shape. The floor was mud, the walls were slabs and posts plastered over with mud, and the roofs were logs covered with yet more mud. Around these rooms were clustered small slab-sided cists with bottle-necked tops made to hold all the earthly possessions of their owners. In one of them we found seven hundred ears of variously colored corn, bright and new, looking as if it had been harvested but yesterday. Whenever we discover something like that—a treasure carefully stored away so long by somebody who left, never returning to uncover its hiding place, I am seized with a great curiosity. Who was it, where did he go, and what tragedy befell him that he never came back for his precious horde?

Ann Morris's book paints a vivid picture of canyon archaeology in the 1920s. I used her words in interpretive programs the previous summer, bringing the image of Ben's grandfather alive for visitors—the clink, clink, clink of a dull metal trowel on canyon rock, a man in a wide-brimmed hat bent over to examine some new find with avid interest.

Ben, Charlie, and I headed toward one of Earl Morris's more remote excavation sites. We carried our lunch and a supply of large white plastic bags to use as boots for crossing the icy wash. Ben shifted his four-wheel drive Toyota into low gear to make it through the soft, sparkling snow. From somewhere in the canyon bottom we heard the tinkling goat bells that were a perennial summer background sound. I had been told there were no flocks in the canyon at this time of year, but I was learning that there were no hard-and-fast rules when it came to the flock's survival. Sure enough, we saw silken mohair goats crossing the roads, leading their less clever cousins, the woolly sheep, to more protected grazing on the canyon floor.

The trail to the bottom was snowy and icy in places. I thought of Noreen's sons, who sometimes used the old trails of carved hand- and toeholds to get from their winter camp on the peninsula to school in Chinle. It was easier for them to hike down one side of the canyon, cross the wash, and hike up the other side than to drive the more than twenty miles of rutted track up the peninsula to the main road.

At the canyon bottom, our first challenge was to cross the wash. We broke through the crust into the mud. In a last effort to keep dry we unrolled the trash bags that covered our boots and pulled them high around our thighs.

In winter, it was possible to imagine how the landscape must have looked for thousands of years, before the erosion control efforts of the US government added tamarisk and Russian olive trees. The dry, teal green of the summer landscape was missing, and trees, stripped by winter frost, were identifiable only by thorns and their placement along the edges of the wash. I thought about a time when only willows and a few cottonwoods lined the bank, and the sandaled feet of the Anasazi climbed the loose rock slopes to their high, dry shelters in the canyon walls.

On the other side of the wash, we broke out of the fog and into the sun, unexpectedly warm after the chill water and shadow of the early morning. We headed up a talus incline to a huge overhang, six hundred feet from the bottom, where Earl Morris and others had excavated in the late 1920s. Charlie was armed with cameras to document some of the eroding rock art on the walls of the deep alcove. Ben brought childhood memories of his mother's tales—her recollections of her parents' stories of digging in the Southwest.

As we climbed, I was aware that, no matter how cautiously I walked, every footstep disturbed the earth and destroyed shards of discarded pottery. On the narrow track we found the prints of horses that clambered up and down the slope. Sheep and goats used the overhang for shelter, unaware that they should not cross the line of vegetation into a designated archaeological site. Grass grew all year around perennial seeps, where water might be gleaned from thick green moss. In the summer these south-facing shelters provide cool shade; in the winter sun they are the keepers of a less forbidding season.

Following the goat track, we reached the edge of the site. The alcove walls were covered with pictographs painted in the same faded teal green as the Russian olives and featuring life-sized figures that bore a close resemblance to the "Wily Coyote" of cartoon fame. Such drawings dated from the Basketmaker period and could be found throughout the canyon. Scholars described them as shamanic figures. The Navajos said they were witches.

Storage cysts from the Basketmaker era lay superimposed over pictographs that had to be even older. We kept outside the line of vegetation while Charlie photographed the drawings for the Park Service collection. In spite of the frigid wash and the snow-covered rim, it was summer in the alcove, as the low rays of the winter sun heated the area to shirtsleeve temperatures.

Over a picnic lunch, we talked about Ben's grandparents and their staff of Navajo field-workers. I wondered how the Navajos might have felt, digging in the shadow of the looming coyote-shamans. We turned to look again at the drawings. It was mid afternoon and the sun had shifted, illuminating the shelter's massive walls with a gentler light. To our amazement, the number of images appeared to have multiplied: figures danced upon figures in a riot of pale green and subtle white. Charlie loaded his camera with infrared film, hoping to capture the changes.

The previous summer, I accompanied a video camera team from Denver to this site. They were making a film about rock art and hauled heavy taping equipment up the steep slope, meandering back and forth across the talus to minimize the arduous climb. While they worked, I explored the site, marveling at the remains of both Basketmaker and Anasazi structures. Among the latter was a deep kiva, about fifteen feet across. At the bottom of the kiva I saw a number of well-aged goat skeletons. They looked like they might have fallen in.

The summer sun had destroyed shooting conditions by midday, so the film crew and I headed back down. Unburdened by equipment, I reached the bottom ahead of the others. An old Navajo man was standing there.

"You go up there?" he asked, extending his lower lip quickly to point at the alcove.

I nodded. "Quite a climb," I told him.

"Them bones still up there?"

I nodded again.

He pointed again. "Sheep go up there, nobody goes after them." He paused. "Used to be other bones up there. Used to be one of those pits was sealed over." He paused again. I waited, hoping for more. He nodded his head twice, then started to move away. "Sheep go up there, nobody goes after them," he said quietly.

Now, as Charlie finished photographing, I walked over to the kiva. It was still filled with the dried skeletons of goats. I took a final look at the looming figures painted on the walls and wondered idly if they got lonely playing guardian to tumbled stone and discarded sandals. A thousand years is a long time to be caught in a story on a canyon wall.

The two weeks of that first winter visit passed quickly. Margarita was busy working and taking care of her father. Her mother, Karen, and her stepfather, Leonard, remained at their peninsula winter camp, where Margarita checked on them frequently. Charlie and I spent some time with the family, but I was still very insecure about the whole fieldwork process and stood by while Margarita tried to explain to her relatives why we wanted to ask questions and take pictures. I was overjoyed when we were invited to join her in some activity, but I didn't push it. I just waited to be asked. As a result, Charlie and I spent a good deal of time hiking in the canyon by ourselves. Driving down the south rim one afternoon after climbing up the White House Trail, we stopped to pick up two "grandmothers"—a popular Navajo term for traditionally dressed older women—who were looking for a ride.

"Going to Basha's," said one, pulling her kerchief close around her head, referring to the supermarket in Chinle. It was hard to tell if she was asking a question or making a statement. Charlie and I had no particular place to be. "We could go to Basha's," I said. Charlie turned to her. "Give you a ride to Basha's and back if I can take a few pictures."

The woman turned to her companion and said something in Navajo. Then she nodded her head in assent. Charlie pulled over to the rim and everybody got out of the car. I took out my notebook and collected names and addresses so that we could get photo releases. Photo session completed, we climbed back into the car and drove toward Basha's. Everybody seemed pleased with the arrangement.

One-time photo opportunities like this were not part of the in-depth process of typical anthropological fieldwork, but working with Charlie taught me about documentation. I learned to frame images with a photographer's eye, just as he had begun asking ethnographic questions with his camera.

When we got back to the duplex, I took out my notebook and started describing the encounter. I covered many pages each day with after-the-fact observations on everything from the texture of the terrain to the feel of the wind in the canyon at dusk. I was careful not to take notes while people were talking to me, which meant that I sometimes sacrificed exact dialogue in the interest of sensitivity. Charlie's cameras were enough of an intrusion into the privacy of canyon residents without me and my notebook hanging on every word.

In part, this decision was a result of my training. My fieldwork professor in graduate school, who had been taught by first- and second-generation anthropologists, told us what they told him: Don't use tape recorders and don't take notes during interviews. Instead, listen quietly while your "informant" is talking, excuse yourself politely every so often, go out to the john, and write it all down verbatim. (This professor also taught us to make two copies of our field notes, a practice I followed for years until I realized his instructions predated the photocopy machine.)

It was almost time to return home. With just one day left, Charlie loaded the cameras, I put my notebooks in my pack, and we joined Margarita for a visit to some clan relatives on the north rim. As we drove along rutted dirt tracks, we talked about the Persian Gulf War and the five canyon men who had already been sent across the sea to fight.

Reaching the homestead, we parked close to where silky angora goats and sheep clustered in a small corral, goat bells and baaing sheep creating a cacophony in the indigo, sunlit morning. Two small houses and an old hogan made up the enclave. Charlie and I waited in the car while Margarita went to the door of one of the houses and talked to the old woman who answered her knock. Once again, I cursed my inability to speak Navajo, feeling like a door-to-door salesperson who couldn't even make her own pitch. Finally Margarita beckoned to us, and we were welcomed into Ida's home.

In the front room two small children—grandkids—played with plastic cars and Ninja Turtles. Ida's daughter sat weaving at a large metal loom made of two-inch pipe welded together to hold rugs up to six feet wide. The family had traded a full-grown sheep for the loom—no small investment. Ida's daughter, who was pregnant with her third child, came out each day from Chinle to weave and to visit with her mother.

Ida was dressed in the traditional fashion: a long, full skirt of red patterned cloth, a purple velveteen shirt with full sleeves, and a silver concho belt. Around her throat were necklaces of silver and turquoise. Only her rubber igloo boots distinguished her garb from that of the nineteenth century.

As a way of explaining what we were doing, Margarita asked me for a copy of the book about New York dairy farms that Charlie and I collaborated on called *Too Wet to Plow.* She handed the book to Ida, who settled down to look at the pictures of black-and-white Holsteins and milk trucks stuck in four-foot snowdrifts. She asked questions about the milking machines and the snow. Charlie took a few pictures and then sat down to warm his hands over the wood stove. I reached into my pack and pulled out a crimson scarf, one of the many I brought to give as gifts to the older women.

Before coming to the canyon, I wrestled with the question of what anthropologists sometimes referred to as "informants' fees." To start, I was uncomfortable with the term "informant," a word I associated with giving away secrets to the FBI or CIA. Moreover, I didn't believe in paying people outright for information. While visiting, we bought food, gas, and other household items, and I selected a few special gifts, like the scarves, to give away. But there had been anthropologists among the Navajos for a hundred years, and some people expected payment. I realized that even on an assistant professor's salary I looked awfully wealthy to the people we visited.

Ida appeared to like the scarf. As we sat together, I could tell that she was joking with me. Her sense of humor was evident in the way she smiled and held herself. Margarita was also enjoying herself, pleased to have an excuse to visit clansfolk long neglected. After a while, Ida turned to Margarita and began to speak slow, melodic Navajo. It was a long speech, the way conversation flows among the Diné, especially in the winter when there's no place you have to be. When she finished talking, she looked away from me.

"You are an educated person and you have been out in the world," Margarita translated, condensing Ida's commentary. "And so you know many things. Can you tell me why this war is happening, what it is all about?"

I tried my best to explain that the Gulf War was a war over resources, much as the coming of the white soldiers to Canyon de Chelly in the 1860s had been. It was not easy, in a house without electricity, without an oil burner, with just the occasional use of a truck, to explain why the biligáana would see fit to fight for oil.

Ida spoke again. "When you go back to your land I want you to tell them something. Say that every morning I get up before the sun rises and I go outside and face the east, and I pray. I pray for the Navajo and all the people involved in this war, that it will be over fast. I do this because your prayers seem not to be working and it is time to give ours a try."

I was silent then, and more than a bit uncomfortable. Charlie caught my eye and grinned. "Are you getting all that, anthropologist?" his expression seemed to say. I nodded at Ida, giving my assent. I would tell as many people as would listen. I agreed with her. I agreed with a lot of what I had begun to learn about the Navajo Way.

"*Hagoonéé',*" Ida said then, the Navajo good-bye that means "see you later" or "good leaving." "Come and visit here again. Next time we'll put you to work!" She reached out her hand to me, and I took it. We touched briefly: the soft, gentle brush that is the Navajo handshake, that says, "I am here, alive, as you are, and I greet you."

During that first year of fieldwork, Charlie and I visited Canyon de Chelly as often as we could. We returned next in late March. It was still snowing in New York, but the Arizona winter is mercifully short, and the thaw had already set in. Once again Margarita met us at the visitor center.

"What are you driving this time?" she asked, eyeing the cars parked at the curb. I tossed my head in the direction of a red subcompact, careful not to use my hands to point. "Geo Metro," I told her. She looked at the car skeptically. "Probably make it," she said.

We were to join her Aunt Noreen's family at DezAh, their winter camp at the far end of the twenty-mile peninsula that divides Canyon de Chelly from Canyon del Muerto. We arrived in late afternoon during a lull between the day's work and dinner. DezAh consisted of two small frame houses, a hogan, corrals, latrines, cooking areas, and shade houses. Noreen, her mother, and her sons occupied one of the houses. Margarita's mother would move into the second when it was completed in late spring.

On the way, Margarita and I talked about Navajo history and how the Diné came to the Southwest. As we joined Noreen, the discussion continued. We compared the history both women had learned from their grandfathers with what I had been taught in anthropology classes.

According to the Navajo origin stories, the Holy People lived in the First, or Black, World, where First Man and First Woman were formed. First Man and First Woman left, along with the Insect Beings, for the Second, or Blue, World, where they encountered animals and birds. There was much sorrow and suffering in the Second World, so they all traveled to the Third, or Yellow World, where Coyote caused a great flood to occur. The Beings were again forced to flee, this time ultimately escaping to the Fourth World through reeds. origin myth

Anthropologists have substituted stories of migration for Navajo tales of emergence. They theorize that people from Asia crossed the Bering Straits land bridge thousands of years ago and trickled into the San Juan River Basin area somewhere between AD 1300 and 1600. Archaeological evidence and early Spanish historical documents link these people with the later Apache and Navajo, whose language, Athapascan, is also spoken by large numbers of people in northwestern Canada and on the Pacific coast. When the Athapascan speakers first arrived in the Southwest they were hunter-gatherers, but by the time they inhabited the lands of north-central New Mexico known as Diné Tah they had become farmers as well as hunters.

During our Park Service orientation, Margarita and I heard a speaker from the Chinle public schools link these two explanations. He told us that traditional Navajo stories supported the land-bridge theory of the anthropologists because they told of the people coming through the reeds. He described a migration in waves and an eventual meeting of the Athapascan peoples with the southwestern Pueblo peoples, the descendants of the Anasazi. The contemporary Navajo people are a product of this meeting, which is why their stories, like those of the Pueblos, speak of creation between the four sacred mountains.

Contact with Pueblo people in the sixteenth century also introduced the Navajos to farming. Over the next hundred years, with the increase in Spanish slave raids and attempts to establish mission settlements in the area, contact between Navajo and Pueblo peoples intensified. In 1680 the Pueblos revolted against the Spanish, and many villagers joined the Navajos in their settlements in Diné Tah, including more than a thousand people from Jemez Pueblo. From the exchanges that took place at this time, the Diné became weavers and pastoralists, acquiring the sheep and horses first brought into the Americas by the Spanish.

The seventeenth and eighteenth centuries were a complex and tumultuous era of forced and forceful cultural exchange. Within a context of warfare and growing pressure on the land, the Navajos left Diné Tah and moved westward into what is now Arizona. By 1730, they crossed the Chuska Mountains and began to settle at Canyon de Chelly. They augmented their basic beliefs and strategies with those of the Pueblos, Spaniards, Mexicans, and Anglos, in turn.

The earliest Navajo homesteads in the canyon included forked-stick hogans, dwellings in which a teepeelike frame of long poles was enclosed with a dried mud covering. These were used until the Navajos were compelled to leave Canyon de Chelly in 1864 as part of the forced march to Fort Sumner, New Mexico, known as the Long Walk. As we started talking about that particular era in recent Navajo history, Noreen turned to Margarita.

"Let's go to Eddie's Overlook!" she said excitedly. Charlie and I looked at them curiously. "It's wonderful, Jeanne," Margarita said. "It

Noreen and extended family view Fortress Rock from Eddie's Overlook.

looks out at Fortress Rock from a different side. Not many biligáana get to see it that way."

I was familiar with Fortress Rock, a tall orange butte located in the deep cut of Black Rock Canyon, and I knew its story. As a consequence of the Mexican-American War of 1846, the Anglos had acquired the northern areas of Mexico, including the Navajo lands. The American Army of the West thereby assumed official control over the citizens of New Mexico territory as well as all Indian tribes within the region.

The relationship between the New Mexicans and the Navajos in the nineteenth century was characterized by constant raiding by both groups—the New Mexicans seeking slaves, the Navajos seeking livestock. According to Army records, between 1846 and 1850 an estimated 800,000 sheep and cattle, and 20,000 horses and mules, were stolen in northwestern New Mexico. Even if these figures were exaggerated, such behavior did not endear the Navajos to Anglos, and in the early 1860s an order was issued to destroy the Navajo "threat" to white settlers. In 1863 Colonel Kit Carson was ordered to begin a full-scale military campaign against the Navajos, including the systematic destruction of their crops and stock.

The decisive move in this campaign was the invasion of Canyon de Chelly in early 1864. The Navajos living there herded sheep and cultivated the fertile lands, their rich cornfields and peach orchards providing a stronghold of food and security. Carson's forces burned the fields and cut down the trees, forcing the surrender of more than two hundred residents.

But not all the Navajo people surrendered. Some took refuge at the top of Fortress Rock. It is said that a woman climbed down each night under cover of darkness to bring food and water to those besieged on its ledges. A precipitous trail leads from the bottom of the butte, with one log ladder visible. Nowadays, the ascent is not possible without the help of ropes and climbing equipment, but the people went up the steep sides and built rough shelters in the hope of outlasting the campaigns of Carson's army.

Noreen's suggestion that we visit the fortress overlook was received with enthusiasm. At about five o'clock, Margarita, Noreen, her three sons, her nephew, a neighbor, Charlie, and I piled into the back of a pale blue pickup driven by Noreen's oldest son, Eddie, and set out for the canyon rim. The road was a solid clay rut, but well traveled and passable for trucks with four-wheel drive and good clearance. A mile or so along, Eddie turned off the road to follow a faint, sandy track into the low blue sage and prickly pear. He parked the truck and we jumped down and began the short walk to the edge. Bobcat had been there before us; a well-rounded set of prints cut clear and deep along the path.

We reached the rim and crowded onto two promontories overhanging the canyon. Sharing binoculars, we leaned out over the edge and tried to see the ladders, trails, and walls in the gathering dusk. Margarita told the story of the siege as she had heard it, some of which was new to Noreen and the boys.

"I wish I'd asked my great-grandpa to tell me the story when he was alive, when these were still living memories," Noreen said with a sigh. "But we were told not to ask questions, not to pry back into the past." She strained to see back into the months of 1864 known as the "fearing time."

The boys were vying for possession of the binoculars, asking Margarita countless questions about whether their relatives had survived the siege on top of the butte. I listened to her answers with interest. We had both learned the official version of the story during Park Service orientation, but Margarita added additional details and pointed out defensive walls and half-fallen structures dating from the occupation period.

"I wish I could go back in time!" Noreen said. "I'm going to think about the fortress before I go to sleep. Maybe I can dream it." Noreen's desire to know more about her people's history was unusual, for it was the way of the older, more traditional Navajo not to recall the times of horror and trial for the Diné. I was learning from Margarita that stories of the recent past were not told unless there was a reason.

Despite these prohibitions, some months after we gathered at the rim of Black Rock Canyon, a group of Navajo rangers and guides made a pilgrimage to Hwééldi, the site of the Bosque Redondo Reservation at Fort Sumner, New Mexico. They wanted to learn firsthand about one of the most ominous chapters in Navajo history.

In the summer of 1863, the first Navajos had been removed to Bosque Redondo. Eventually, 8,000 were marched across the Southwest, a 370- to 470-mile trek. Most were near starvation at the outset, and casualty rates along the way were more than ten percent.

The Army planned to set up a series of farming villages at Bosque Redondo using irrigation agriculture, but the crops failed, the livestock died, and smallpox killed more than 2,000 people. The Navajos were starving, forced to depend on meager government provisions to stay alive. By 1868, thousands had died or disappeared in an attempt to return to their homelands in the west. Finally, a treaty was negotiated between the US and the designated "chiefs," allowing those who survived to live on lands to the west set aside as a reservation. Comprising about one-fourth of their original territory, the region ended just west of Chinle. In 1868, the Navajos of Canyon de Chelly began the walk back home.

The young Navajos from Canyon de Chelly who traveled to Fort Sumner in 1991 felt it was time to see the place known to them from oral history and to make offerings. "I needed to know about this. My children should know about this," said Chad Benally, a longtime ranger. Margarita was ambivalent when she heard about the visit. "I couldn't go there intentionally," she told me. "But if I passed near, I would stop."

One of the older men was vehement. "They should not have gone there," he insisted. "These things are best forgotten."

Chapter 2

Blue Sky Morning

"It's my first day at sheep camp, and I can't find the sheep!" Noreen said as she looked around in amazement, her hands on her hips. She was standing in front of her mother's two-room house at DezAh, wearing blue jeans and a heavy jacket partly zipped against the early spring chill. Noreen had spent the winter with an aunt in Chinle, but her older sons often stayed at DezAh to see the herd through the cold, snowy months.

After the deaths of her husband and her father five years before, Noreen and her children had taken over full responsibility for the family sheep herd. For the boys this was a delight; they loved the animals and the canyon, and moved easily from playing high school football to herding. Noreen worked hard with the sheep while cooking and keeping her mother's houses as open havens for many family members. She was also a traditional dancer who performed at winter ceremonies and at competitions in the spring. Though steeped in traditional Navajo life, she was always curious about the world beyond the reservation.

"How was it here this winter?" I asked Eddie, Noreen's oldest son. "Snow was pretty deep," he said. "We used hand- and toe-hold trails most of the time. Couple of weeks ago they were covered with ice. What a climb! We made it okay."

On foot, the trip from DezAh to the south rim was about six miles, by truck or car at least fifty. Today the ruts were dry and solid, turning the route into a four-lane dirt thoroughfare that eventually led to the family enclave. In the corral there were a number of newborn lambs and goats, all legs and voice, no more than a week old. One of these was a special black lamb, a birthday gift from Noreen to Eddie.

"Come look at that lamb!" Noreen said to Charlie and me. "I bought it in town and put it in the corral one night with a red ribbon around its neck and a sign saying 'I'm yours.'" The black lamb mingled with the

31

other newborns, who stumbled around the corral looking for a mom and an udder. Eddie smiled as he went toward him, baby bottle in hand.

A lot of sheep had been lost, some to the weather, others to *maa'ii*, marauding coyotes. Many of the older sheep were still missing, and the boys saddled up their horses to begin a search. They moved carefully down the slope into a side canyon, sending the straggling goats and sheep back to the corral. I followed on foot and waited just above a small reservoir filled with winter melt. There was a sudden noise behind me. Seven sheep and one lamb came bounding down the slick rock to drink. One of the boys was right behind them, and he dismounted quickly. He removed the horse's bridle for a few moments to allow it to drink before everyone headed up the tumbled stone in the direction of home.

The sun was sinking fast, and back at the house there were people busy everywhere. Margarita had twelve sisters, each with a family of her own. It was not uncommon to find more than forty people gathered for an evening meal.

Moving back into the camp meant repairing whatever had not survived the winter. Most of the family lived on the rim from September to April so that the children could get to school each day. But the school year would soon be over, and the children would be expected to spend time herding the sheep that were now grazing on the early spring grass. In a few weeks the flock would be moved to the canyon bottom, and the family would move with it.

Karen and Leonard at the housewarming for Karen's new house at DezAh.

Margarita and I walked over to her mother's newly completed house. Fifteen years ago a federal housing program provided funds to build new homes for the Navajos of Canyon de Chelly. Karen, Margarita's mother, did the required paperwork to qualify for the program. Then she waited— for fifteen years. At last she got a letter from the housing program: her paperwork had been found, and she was still eligible for a new home! The house was built, and just blessed the previous week. Family and friends brought gifts; Karen's daughters chipped in to buy a bedroom suite and other furnishings.

The new house was a small, three-roomed structure, fully wired and plumbed in accordance with US Department of Housing and Urban Development specifications. Margarita and I looked at it and laughed. The nearest electricity and water were six miles away, on the south rim of the canyon, and it was unlikely that these services would reach the peninsula any time soon.

We turned away from the new home to begin cleanup on a log-and-brush shade house that hadn't survived the winter. Snow had broken the main cross beams, and the roof cover of small, leafy tree limbs had tumbled to the ground. The loose branches needed to be cleared from the cracked beams and dragged close to a fire pit near Karen's house. Margarita cut a broom of woody sagebrush and I grabbed an ancient rake whose wooden handle had been replaced with a length of durable half-inch pipe; it was heavy but still functional after years of maintenance. The smell of sage enveloped us as we swept the loose leaves into the center of the roofless shade house. Soon it was replaced by the familiar incense of burning leaves.

"When I was a kid in Brooklyn, we used to burn great piles of leaves between parked cars," I told Margarita. "I love the smell."

"Have you always lived in cities, Jeanne?" she asked. I was learning that the details of my life were as curious and exotic to Margarita and her family as theirs was to me.

"Always," I answered, "until I started teaching in Oneonta. We had a ten-by-twenty-foot backyard, but we still grew tomatoes and grapes."

The sun was sinking fast and the temperature was falling. We finished our cleanup and joined the rest of the group gathered around a welcoming fire between the corral and the house where Ellen, Noreen's mother, lived. I could hear the rhythmic slap, slap, slap of bread being formed into rounds to be fried in a waiting pan of hot Crisco. (It was called "bread"— never "fry bread." If the same dough was baked over the fire, the flat rounds were called "tortillas.")

We began a hubbub of cooking to feed the family—at least twenty women and children and a few men—who arrived from scattered tasks across the peninsula. The fire was white-hot and cluttered with pans.

Cooking mutton over an open fire.

Browning onions and ground beef, I was forced to step back periodically when the flames grew too hot.

"You're not used to cooking over an open fire, are you?" asked Margarita's cousin, Barbara. I shook my head. "You mean you don't feel this heat like I do?" "Nope," said Barbara, turning a piece of bread with a long, forked stick. "You get used to it, just like you get used to heat in summer."

It was getting dark and cold, and we decided to move indoors for dinner. We squeezed around tables close to Ellen's wood stove. Though there was a plank floor in the main room, the dining area floor was dirt, covered with carpet. Floorboards, and plasterboard for the ceiling, would have to wait until the sale of a rug or some other windfall provided cash that could go beyond immediate, day-to-day needs. Dishes, cups, bowls, knives, and forks were set down next to the large pots of steaming stew and hot bread. Children scampered about everywhere, but there was remarkably little chaos or crying. Nobody demanded extra attention or yelled "I want, I want . . . ," as happened whenever little kids got together at my house. The food was served against an undertone of comment from some of the women, who took note of whose children ate first and how much.

Before dinner, at Noreen's insistence, Charlie said an opening grace, a Christian prayer that he barely remembered but that Noreen recited without a pause. After the meal, Ellen concluded with a blessing. Rubbing her fingers on her breast and knees, she asked the Holy Ones to make her limbs strong with the good food.

Her prayer translated, Ellen welcomed us into her home and thanked us for sharing food. Then she surprised us by asking Charlie and me to talk to the boys and girls about what it takes to grow up in the white world—what they would need to know to survive, and how important it was to have a good education. With wood smoke and the crisp Arizona air drifting through the room, such things seemed insignificant. In my own home, I would have asked Ellen to tell my children how important it was to listen to the wind, to walk without fear under the blue sky, to live in harmony with all of nature. I didn't know how to start. Noreen came to my rescue by asking if I had been a hippie. I talked about how I dropped out of school and why I decided to complete my education when I was older.

It was late. The older boys piled into pickup trucks and returned to town in preparation for the new school week. The rest of us pulled the tables and benches outside and covered the dirt floor with huge pieces of foam, turning most of the room into a bed. The littlest kids, already sound asleep, were covered with blankets wherever they happened to rest. The cry from the other children was "Tell us a story!"—the plea that sets the stage for long, dark evenings all around the world.

Here, at the confluence of winter and springtime, it was still proper to tell the cold-weather tales, so Noreen began to speak of Coyote and of eerie lights shining in the distance with no apparent source. Because this was the twentieth century, we speculated about UFOs, but for the most part we talked about Navajo witches, shape-shifting, and "skinwalkers," beings who could change their form by donning the skins of dead animals and humans.

"What do you think?" Noreen asked me. "Do you believe in UFOs and any of the things we've been talking about?" Before answering I thought about my aging mother. In recent years, she had retreated into a world of her own, inhabited by people and creatures I couldn't see. "Sometimes I think there's a lot more out there than I've seen myself," I said.

Belief in things the Anglo world deems supernatural is part of the day-to-day fabric of Navajo life. In the interdependence of all living things, such beings are regarded as other members of the natural world. Navajo religious belief is a philosophy of life. It is medicine, literature, history, and ethics all at once. It is the Navajo Way. The oral accounts of emergence—of the journey to this Fourth and glittering world—are the history of the people. In the stories of the elders, in the songs of the medicine men, is the knowledge needed to move in the circle of life, to walk in beauty or in harmony with all the beings of this universe.

Hózhóní, the notion of beauty as well-being, balance, and order, is at once a goal, a state, and a blessing. It is the essential character of all things dwelling well together—attainable and yet subject to displacement. Thus, special songs and ceremonies can be performed to realign disordered forces and regain a lost center in order to live each day in an ecology of self and world as one.

The very nature of some individuals calls them to assist the rest of the people in maintaining essential harmony. They are the *hataalii*, or singers, who go through arduous training to become keepers of portions of the total song. Each singer masters a ceremony intended to reinstate harmony disrupted by specific causes. In a rapidly changing world, the potential causes of disruption are multiplying. For instance, contact with an enemy requires a ceremony to reinstate harmony. At one time, an enemy was fairly easy to identify. Today, the range of things that could be classified as enemies is increasing, and the category is not as clear-cut as it once was.

The significant time and training required to become a singer have limited the number of persons available to conduct ceremonies. At the same time, many older Navajos are concerned that the traditional ceremonies are not adequate to present-day situations and perhaps should not be passed on in the form that was healing in the last century. The blessings, after all, were designed for a people who traveled on foot or on horseback, accompanying their herds.

According to Margarita, Noreen's mother, Ellen, possessed knowledge of prayers, ceremonies, and sacred sites that she never shared with her younger relatives. "I asked her about Dog Rock, down by the junction, but she wouldn't tell me," Margarita said. "She said she wasn't sure whether she should pass on what she had learned from her mother. She said she didn't know if the ceremonies would work anymore."

"What do you mean?" I asked. Margarita paused. "Well, for instance, if Coyote walks across your path, we have prayers. You say 'Bless these legs that I walk on; bless this horse that I'm riding on.' But could I say the same words with the same results if Coyote passed right now? 'Bless this Chevy S10 Blazer'?"

I laughed, but she was right. Catholics have changed the liturgy and practice of the Mass to keep up with the times. Why shouldn't Navajos make changes as they see fit? Traditional Navajo practices have endured in spite of, and in concert with, attempts by Christian religions to impose their beliefs through schools, missions, medical facilities, and social welfare agencies. Many Navajos who consider themselves Christians and attend Christian church services also participate in Navajo ceremonies or belong to the Native American Church. As elsewhere in the world, the coming of organized religion did not obliterate the practice of age-old traditional beliefs.

"We will dam up the river of gold flowing through the reservation," said former Navajo Nation president Peterson Zah while on a visit to

Chinle in 1992. The occasion was a ribbon-cutting ceremony at the site of the old Garcia's Trading Post, a pink adobe-and-faced-stone structure that burned down in the 1970s. For three-quarters of a century it had been a place to trade, sell rugs, and buy supplies. During the two decades that Garcia's remained empty, the Park Service presented elaborate plans to increase the size of its visitor center by building on the historic site. But in early April 1992, a sign went up on the lot: "Jobs for your community. Future home of the new Chinle Hotel. Developers: Division of Economic Development, Ocean Properties Limited." Holiday Inn was on its way to Canyon de Chelly.

The community split over the prospect of change. Like Chinle's other hotels, this one would charge rates that rivaled those in major cities. The "river of gold" Peterson Zah referred to—money spent by tourists on hotels and restaurants—would flow to the development corporation, not to community members. There are, in fact, few places in Chinle where tourist dollars wind up in Navajo hands.

Nevertheless, the potential for jobs generated excitement. Margarita's cousin, a man who worked at the coal mines near Kayenta, ninety miles away, applied for a carpenter's position, one of the few created during the construction period. Another hundred service jobs maids—wait staff, maintenance, and a few management positions—would become available when the hotel opened. A three-month training program, covering skills from serving coffee to operating computers, prepared a number of local residents for guaranteed employment.

Noreen and Alicia, one of Margarita's sisters, were included in the training program. "We were up at the employment office looking for jobs, and we saw a sign announcing the training," Noreen told us. "It was starting that afternoon so we went right over. You had to have applications in long before, but somehow we talked our way in."

Her enthusiasm showed in her eyes and her voice. "I love learning new things. It's good to be in school again after so many years."

We were sitting in the Elite Laundromat at the Tsegi Shopping Center in Chinle. Charlie had bought a rug from Noreen, one of the first she'd made in years, and we drove her in from the peninsula to buy groceries, do laundry, and shop for birthday gifts for her older sons.

Before nine in the morning was the best time to wash clothes at the Elite. You had your choice of functioning machines, the dryers were empty, and the aisles were free of the usual throng of kids. Two young girls were reading the glossy ads in the Navajo Times, a free weekly newspaper. Both wore canvas slip-on shoes from the variety store next door, where a going-out-of-business sale was moving into its fourth month. Their T-shirts and shorts, the "official" costume of young Navajoland as soon as spring arrived, were in sharp contrast to the colorful velveteens of the two grandmothers standing by a triple-loader in the center of the laundromat. KTNN, "hit-kicking country voice of the Navajo Nation," provided a bilingual accompaniment to the gear-on-gear noises of the machines. The wash had finished. Charlie looked into the machine and commented that there were still suds.

"Well," said Noreen, laughing, "at the Elite you don't have to worry if you don't have money to buy soap! At least the water is clear, different from the all-night laundry at the convenience store. Their sign says 'Wash at your own risk,' the water's so brown."

We transferred the clothes to the dryer and walked over to Basha's to buy coffee and chicken. Basha's is a supermarket, feed and tack shop, and bakery—a high-priced monopoly, like most stores on the reservation. It carried mutton and huge sacks of Bluebird flour for Navajo customers, easy-cook barbecue items for tourists, and tofu and gourmet coffee for the young doctors and nurses at the Indian Health Service Hospital.

Over in the third aisle, where the toy section spilled onto the floor, a handful of kids were playing with cars and dolls and puzzles. Store employees never reprimanded the youngsters; evidently, it was an unwritten policy to provide this child-care service while mothers shopped. Noreen bought a shirt for one of her boys, and we returned to the parking lot. At this hour, it too was quiet. The yellow snowplow parked at the entrance was testimony to the blinding sandstorms that blow in periodically, limiting visibility and throwing flying sand into eyes, teeth, and just-washed laundry. The red-eyed men lounging at the entrance to Basha's attested to a different type of storm whipping through the reservation, where the dark winds of joblessness, alcohol, and desperation tore through some families and communities.

I turned to Noreen. In addition to the packages she carried, she had just ordered two sheet cakes for the joint birthday celebration. "You spent just about all that Charlie paid you for the rug on your boys, didn't you?" I asked. I knew how much she cared for her sons. "Yes," she said, smiling shyly. "They're gonna be so surprised!"

Noreen's sons seemed to be doing all right. There was some question about whether Eddie would finish high school, but he was a hard worker who preferred working in the canyon to sitting in a classroom. I wondered how he and the other canyon boys would fare in the years to come.

The slow demise of the herding economy over the past half-century, combined with the failure to introduce jobs and the values associated with wage labor, created unemployment rates on the reservation far above the national average. No family seemed able to escape the waves of alcohol abuse that gripped men and women trying desperately to mesh the beliefs and philosophy of their grandparents' generation with the consumer lifestyle driving mainstream America. It was especially difficult for those approaching middle age—a generation that was slightly removed from the memory and practice of the old ways and had been educated in a climate of boarding schools and BIA policies that stressed assimilation.

Since the late 1960s, reservation schools have written their own curricula in an attempt to integrate the skills needed to survive in the technological morass of the contemporary world with the knowledge needed to transcend it. At Tsaile, at the eastern end of Canyon de Chelly, Diné College provides higher education in a setting that allows young people and those returning to school to get the skills they need without leaving their families and all that is familiar.

Although this is a beginning, culturally sensitive economic development has yet to occur on the Navajo Reservation. Most industries and businesses in the region are parasitic, taking resources and money out of the area and ignoring the long-term needs of the Navajo Nation. High-level jobs in industry, education, and health are generally staffed by non-Navajos. While the tribe struggles to produce its own professionals, it is a slow process aimed at the youth. Those in their middle years are left to flounder between two worlds.

Nor are young people who are educated and working off the reservation immune to the dilemma. One of my fellow park rangers in 1990, an anthropology major married to a biligáana, returned to Canyon de Chelly for the summer from her home in Phoenix. "Who *are* you?" her grandmother asked her one day. "I don't recognize you." She returned to the Park Service housing in tears.

Another young woman went east to study archaeology at an Ivy League college. She returned to work in the canyon with Park Service archaeologists. Her grandmother was startled at the effect the long eastern winter had on her granddaughter's appearance. It wasn't until the end of the summer, after weeks of working in the sun, that the girl's grandmother was satisfied. "Now you look like the girl I remember," she said.

Cable TV accomplished in just a few years what decades of educational policy and missionization could not. The message and lifestyle broadcast in sitcoms and commercials not only sell goods but also plants goals that differ from those valued in the past. Yet many Navajos remain unsure of how much of the bounty of technology they want to accept. Margarita and I talked often about whether it was possible to acquire skills from the white world without losing sight of what it meant to be Navajo. Some of those caught between desires for the "stuff" of technology and the harmony of their basic beliefs fill the gulf with alcohol.

Tribal law makes it illegal to sell and consume alcoholic beverages within the Navajo Nation. Consequently, "border towns" such as Gallup, New Mexico, and Flagstaff, Arizona, have become tragic magnets for the kind of uncontrolled drinking that grows out of hopelessness and frustration. On the reservation itself, alcohol is available from bootleggers. A constant battle is waged between Navajo tribal police and people involved in illegal sales. Beyond these official struggles is the sorrow of families as they watch members succumb to alcoholism.

The last few years have seen an upsurge in attempts to change this picture. A drive for legalization of alcohol sales within the reservation is sparked by twin concerns. Legalization would put an end to the money-draining bootlegging business and would eliminate the long and often lethal drives to the reservation border and back to drink. A visible movement toward sobriety is fostered by agencies such as Alcoholics Anonymous as well as the Native American Church (NAC). Most striking, however, are the changes coming from the people themselves through the formation of self-help groups.

Charlie sometimes grew impatient with the long pauses between activities. He hadn't quite adjusted to Navajo time—beginning the day with one intent and seeing it flow in entirely unexpected directions. I was a little more comfortable with the uneven, unpredictable pace, having come of age in the 1960s with a basic understanding that "wherever you go, there you are." In the canyon, you might start out in the morning on the way to a sheep-shearing, stop to pick someone up along the route, make a quick diversion to fetch the shears thirty miles away, pick up a couple of kids after school, realize it's time for dinner, make bread for twenty-five, finish cleanup in the dark, grab a sleeping bag for the night, and finally locate the sheep sometime the next morning.

Easter weekend dawned clear and blue. All along the peninsula families were gathering to celebrate the reawakening of the land through a Christian-based celebration. Because April is a busy month for the Navajos, Easter weekend was a good time to pause and share food and fun with relatives. The sheep and goats that survived the cold in their winter camp corrals would soon be moved to the canyon bottom, where new grass followed close on the heels of the melting snow. Their thick wool coats served them well over the past months, but must be shorn—a contribution to the local economy, and the beginning of the new cycle of growth and regeneration.

Noreen had her own flock to shear, but one of the neighboring grandmothers offered to pay five dollars per animal to get her sheep and goats done quickly. Gathering every pair of shears they could find, the family drove a few miles east to another enclave. When Charlie and I arrived there were six people inside the corral, and the children were helping to herd Angora goats into the enclosure.

Red baling twine wrapped around the horns tethered each goat to the rail, but it took a lot more to keep it still for the shearing. The young ones balked and bleated; it was their first time and they didn't understand what

Angora goat round-up: Margarita and Everett.

was going on. Noreen, Margarita, and two of Margarita's sisters each grabbed a tethered goat, keeping them quiet by holding the animals between their legs. The double-bladed pressure shears made a dull, metallic click as they cut the matted wool close to the animal's skin. The blades were soaked in a healing extract of juniper and sage, a precautionary medicine in case the skin was broken.

In the center of the corral, a ram was tethered to a bulky juniper that had been cut down and made into a table. A young man, black hair flowing to the middle of his back, worked steadily. He was alternately shearing and swearing at the uncooperative ram, whose feet were tied together with more red twine. A baseball cap protected the man's head from the heat of the morning sun, and as he cut, the children packed the wool into an empty lettuce crate for shipping. Traders were paying sixty cents a pound for angora wool. At those prices it was difficult to figure out how any profit could be made from its sale.

The little children chattered incessantly in two languages, goading their mothers with cries of "Aren't you done with that one yet?" As each goat was finished, the shearer stood, stretched, and groaned, pulling the kinks out of her lower spine. It was backbreaking work that seemed endless. Once released, the pink-skinned animals were driven out of the corral and the children chased new goats toward the workers. The rich, oily smell of lanolin permeated the air and saturated the clothes and skin of anyone coming near.

Margarita's sister finishes shearing.

Just after noon we went up to the house for lunch: mutton stew and delicious bread. A four-year-old brought water to the table by siphoning it with a rubber hose from a silver polyurethane barrel taller than he was. Everyone who worked got to eat, but the crew disappeared quickly after lunch to avoid being asked to start shearing sheep. Sheep wool grows tightly and is often more tangled than that of goats. It was time-consuming and more difficult work. Besides, back at Noreen's house there were tens of dozens of hard-boiled eggs waiting to be dyed for the Easter celebration.

As we prepared to leave, Margarita looked at the small flock of sheep. "My father told me about the time when my great-grandfather came home from herding bursting with great joy. It was spring, the sheep had lambed, and the family now had close to a thousand animals. 'Now we are truly rich!' he told everybody. We always reckoned prosperity by the size of the flock."

This feeling was prevalent on the reservation in the years prior to 1933, when Navajo "traditional" life was defined by the relationship between people, land, and animals in a herding economy. The Navajos who came back from Bosque Redondo in 1868—a total of fewer than 9,000—had been granted land amounting to ten percent of their original territory. Returning too late to plant crops, they relied on government rations for the first few years. Under treaty provisions, they also received 14,000 sheep and 1,000 goats, which they drove to good forage, often outside reservation boundaries. By 1876, land equal to twice the reservation acreage was occupied by those living off-reservation. Five additions were made to the reservation between 1878 and 1886, bringing the total acreage to 11.5 million.

Schools and trading posts began springing up. Indian agents encouraged the people to produce and sell wool and wool products and, by the 1890s, herds had grown to more than 1.5 million animals. The human population was growing as well, from the almost 9,000 who returned from Bosque Redondo to 20,000 in 1900.

The traders and trading posts brought Anglo ways and products to the reservation, as did the establishment of Bureau of Indian Affairs (BIA) boarding schools between 1900 and 1913. Though only a small number of Navajo children attended, BIA schooling was supplemented by religious organizations that opened missions, schools, and hospitals on the reservation. By 1930, the reservation had expanded to 14,360,000 acres and was home to 40,000 Navajos and 1,297,589 sheep and goats—an average of about thirty-two animals per capita. Today, the total number of animals is only 317,388, while human population is estimated at 165,065—slightly less than two animals for each Navajo.

This drastic reduction in livestock was a consequence of neither natural disaster nor Navajo desire. In 1933, the United States government asked the tribe to join with livestock holders throughout the West in a program of mandated stock reduction designed to control overgrazing and soil erosion. The program was beneficial to stockholders with large herds, who were able to get rid of unproductive stock, but it caused hardship to those with small flocks. The Navajos expressed little overt hostility, although they found it hard to imagine how wage labor could replace the wealth and security of livestock.

The immediate reduction quota of 400,000 for the reservation was achieved by 1934. Government conservation and soil-erosion control initiatives provided a source of short-term income for many men, giving the illusion of a developing cash economy. In Canyon de Chelly, where the national monument had been established in 1931, men were hired to build dams and plant Russian olive and tamarisk trees. But it soon became apparent that the necessary wage labor simply did not exist anywhere on the reservation. Equally clear was the intrinsic difference between money and wealth. For the Navajos, wages could never provide wealth in the same way that the sheep and goats had done.

A second process of herd reduction was proposed in 1934. This time, the primary goal was the elimination of 150,000 goats. The government's drought relief program provided the funds to purchase the animals, which were to be driven to central shipping locations near the railroad. Bad weather and long distances hampered this scheme. The Navajos pressed the government to be allowed at least to slaughter the animals for food, a request that was granted but later withdrawn. Ultimately, huge numbers of

goats were killed and left to rot. This round of reductions bred intense bitterness among the Navajo people, and subsequent programs could be accomplished only through the use of government force. Not until 1954 was the tribe permitted to regulate its livestock industry. Even now, decades later, the experience of the 1930s remains vivid in the minds of many Navajos.

Although the outright reduction programs ended, other methods were instituted to control the relationship between sheep and land. Ceilings on the size of individual flocks were accompanied by the designation of grazing districts, which required that people limit their movement to a circumscribed area. No one could own sheep without a permit, and no one could hold more than 350 sheep or goats. In counting the size of the herd, a formula was devised in which one horse equaled five sheep and one cow equaled four. Each family group was assigned a customary use area, its size determined by the number of livestock they were permitted.

Today, the Navajo people recall these events with the same sadness they feel about the Long Walk. The decline of the herding economy affected not only the herders but also everyone whose livelihood was related to the keeping of sheep and the production of wool and wool products. Wage labor did not expand to take up the slack, nor was the Anglo work ethic easily accepted. For many Navajos, nothing could match the joy of watching young lambs cavort in leaps and bounds, bleating and baaing behind a tolerant ewe.

"You're Italian aren't you?" Noreen asked hesitantly. It was the evening of Easter Sunday, and we were standing in the mauve-and-eggshell dusk feeding Eddie's black lamb. I nodded, yes. "Is it true . . . ," Noreen began again. "I mean . . . we hear that Italians eat young sheep, even before they give their first wool." I nodded again in confirmation. Noreen shook her head in disbelief. "How awful. How can anyone kill the babies?" she asked.

I looked at her. I never really thought about it before. My family had always eaten lamb, delicately seasoned with garlic and roasted to perfection. Though my grandparents herded sheep outside of Naples, we were now city folks, and there was no relationship between the animal, *sheep*, and the food, *lamb*. "I never saw them as babies, Noreen. I only saw them as meat. But outside New York City, farmers raise lambs just for Easter dinner," I told her.

We had just finished an Easter feast of mutton stew. This was no baby sheep that filled the dinner pot. Tough as usual, cooked for hours, this was some member of the flock that had done a final service for the family by becoming dinner.

Opposite page: Goats entering canyon.

Because it was the first holiday period of the good weather, Easter weekend was a high visitation time for Southwestern monuments. The campground at de Chelly was already full and the visitor center busy, but there were no official ranger activities scheduled. The sun was warm and brilliant on Easter Sunday, as I walked to DezAh on the heavily traveled White House Trail. In my uniform, I would be identified as a Park Service representative and available to answer visitor questions.

The trail drops 600 feet from the south rim to the canyon bottom. It is well maintained, and everyone from babies to seniors with canes can be found navigating its many switchbacks. Children usually hit the trail running; Navajo kids know the secret routes and clamber across the russet sandstone in seemingly impassable places. On this Easter morning, I found myself walking behind five young Mennonite women wearing blue-and-pink polyester and carrying white purses. They were gabbing and laughing, their dresses swaying in the aggressive April wind. Watching them, I thought about the simplicity of their lives compared to most of the other canyon visitors.

We greeted each other and they asked a few questions about the White House Ruin. The wash was running with the fierceness of a mountain stream, and crossing was no easy task. But they rolled up their dresses and waded quickly through the chilly water. I rolled up my pants and followed close behind. As we stood in front of the 1,000-year-old structure, waiting for our clothes to dry, they told me about their mission work that provided care for young children in the border town of Gallup. Like many visitors, they were disappointed to find that White House Ruin was fenced and could not be entered. I explained that without fences, the fragile buildings would be destroyed by heavy boot soles and souvenir-seeking tourists.

We marveled together at the blueness of the springtime sky. The new buds on the tamarisk and Russian olive trees made the canyon edge a pale band of dusty pink and green, so different from the heat-drained green of summer.

I continued alone down the canyon, moving in and out of the chill water of the wash. With each new season the wash cut a new course, carving the sand banks into microcanyons of their own. I looked carefully at the new walls, watching for the artifacts that often emerge as the waters recede. I was headed for the Yei Trail, an ingenious series of hand- and toe-holds created by the Anasazi and now used by the Navajos to get from the canyon bottom to the peninsula. Metal handrails and cables had been added along a good portion of the trail.

The holds were filled with loose sand blown in during the winter, which I swept clean for the next person as I climbed. Navajos traverse these trails as if they were level sidewalks, encouraged from toddlerhood to perfect the climbing that is an essential skill in canyon country. Horses and sheep are brought up and down many of the trails as well, and the remains of ancient log ladders survive after centuries of maintenance and repair.

At the top of the trail I followed a dirt track the last three miles to Noreen's house. A well-used purple Easter basket was blowing through the wildflowers and sage along the road. I tossed it over my arm and continued, anticipating the giant Easter-egg hunt scheduled to take place later in the day. At DezAh, Charlie had just arrived by car and family members began to show up carrying three or four cartons of colored eggs, as well as candy, soda pop, and other small items to be used as prizes in the hunt.

Dinner was being prepared at Ellen's house. The women were already making bread. The two sheet cakes from Basha's had arrived, commemorating both Easter and the birthdays of Noreen's oldest sons. Sheet cakes were a central part of almost every celebration within driving distance of the bakery, and there were seldom leftovers.

In the cooking area, I picked up a hunk of dough and started trying to shape bread. Margarita's mother, Karen, one of five grandmothers present for the occasion, greeted me jokingly. "Look at her," she said in Navajo, "She just walked all the way across the canyon without getting tired, and now she's making bread. If she was my daughter-in-law she probably wouldn't be doing anything!" Her daughter Lora translated. Laughing, I poked the customary hole in the bread, dropped it in the oil, and returned Karen's hug.

Outside the house there were already as many children and adults as there were dozens of eggs, and more kept arriving. Similar celebrations were taking place all along the peninsula and in the canyon itself as people gathered to commemorate the end of winter.

Margarita was given the job of organizing the hunt, designating the prizes, and hiding forty dozen eggs. While the eggs were hid, the men and boys practiced roping, and a brisk debate took place concerning the order of the day's events: food or fun? Deciding to eat first, the men carried tables outside the house, and a serving line formed in front of pots of stew, soup, and bread. Charlie contributed a bowl of potatoes au gratin, for which he had become famous in Margarita's family. Karen said a blessing for all, for the bounty of the food, the gift of good company, and the new season. As everyone filled up, Margarita slipped away and finished hiding the prize eggs, each marked with a number corresponding to a particular prize.

"Auntie, when can we do the hunt?" several of the children cried, eating cake with one hand and holding Easter baskets in the other.

The eggs were hidden in two areas, one for the younger children, the other for the teens and adults. There were ten prize eggs for each group, with a grand prize of ten dollars. Everyone lined up at the edge of the field of competition—a stand of high, fragrant sagebrush. The older men were in dress shirts, wide-brimmed black hats, and western boots, and the grandmothers wore their best satins and velveteens, turquoise and silver around their necks and waists. They provided an impressive contrast to the jeans and T-shirts worn by everybody else. All were equipped with containers, from multicolored commercial straw baskets to plastic pickle buckets.

Margarita quieted the crowd, dropped her arm, and yelled "Go!" Forty or more men, women, and children ran into the sage, pushing aside branches to find the hidden eggs. Cries of delight signaled the discovery of each prize egg, and everybody's baskets began to fill. One of the marvels of the Easter-egg hunt was the aftermath, when people actually ate and enjoyed hard-boiled eggs. Here, I thought, was a true cultural difference—five hundred eggs that wouldn't start to smell two weeks after the thrill of coloring them was gone.

Later, while a softball game got under way beyond the sheep corral, Margarita and I sat quietly to one side talking about the meaning of Christian Easter. "Where do the rabbit and the eggs come in? What do they have to do with Christ?" she wondered. "They go back to pre-Christian fertility festivals and celebrations of the coming of spring. In church, Christians celebrate the resurrection of Christ. I guess that afterward they're still celebrating the beginning of the new season of growth," I told her, thinking of the confused syncretism of most contemporary Christian celebrations.

"Well, we've always had big gatherings at Easter, even though we weren't Christians. And we do gifts at Christmas as well," Margarita said. "That must get pretty expensive." Margarita shook her head. "Not really. We draw names and just get a gift for that person."

We walked over to where the women were completing the monumental task of washing the dishes and pots and storing the leftover food. In the main room of the house, the grandmothers cleared the floor and pulled out the equipment for stick dice, an ancient game of chance and skill going back at least as far as the tale of the Great Gambler—the story of how some of the Anasazi came to be. People searched for nickels and pennies to wager, and Margarita's sister Alicia laid out the circle of small stones that was the playing field. The dice were made of long ovals of wood painted on one side, two black and two white. A player held them together in one hand, banged them against a large central stone, and then dropped them. How they fell—two black, two white, one black, one white—determined how far the player moved around the circle.

The grandmothers and a few men stood around the playing area, wedged between a bed and the wood stove, and kids were draped everywhere. The game began in a spirit of hot competition and good humor. Before each turn, the players called for the maximum points often, closing their eyes, tapping the dice, and repeating the Navajo word for ten—

Easter egg hunt, DezAh.

neeznáá. As the game progressed, the banter among the women flowed. It was clear even to a non-Navajo speaker that the commentary was becoming increasingly bawdy. I could read it in the twinkling of Karen's dark eyes and the roars of laughter from those around me.

Outside, the softball game entered its umpteenth inning while the sun sank low in the sky. Each hit sent the ball scurrying into low cactus, between the junipers, into the sheep dung. The runners headed for home plate, bringing in two runs with each hit, but nobody knew the score. Charlie hit a hard one out to Margarita, who had joined the game. The ball hit her hand and jammed her thumb. She let out a yell but threw the ball anyway, and he was out at home plate. As the game ended, people began to head toward their pickups, carrying tired children through the twilight, eggs in hand. For most, there would be school or work the next morning.

American holidays, designed for observance by a working population, are neatly confined to weekends or a single designated day. Navajo ceremonies could last as long as nine days and were held when they were needed, within broad seasonal boundaries. In the past, gathering clansfolk for the prescribed period was not difficult. No one had to be at work by eight o'clock on Monday morning. With the advent of wage labor, however, even a four-day ceremony, two days longer than a weekend, became a problem. Traditional practice began to conflict with the expectations of mainstream employment.

Such was the case with *Kinaaldá*, the puberty ceremony for young women held when a girl began to menstruate. The first Kinaaldá was performed for Changing Woman, the child raised by First Man and First Woman. On the first day of the ceremony, the girl is bathed and dressed in beautiful clothes, her hair tied with buckskin. After that, she begins grinding yellow and white corn into cornmeal. On the second morning, the girl who "walks into beauty" must get up before the sun and run into the east. Joined by her young relatives, she runs across the mesa laden with jewelry, gifts from her grandmothers who instruct her in proper behavior. Then she returns to camp to perform specified duties that teach her physical, moral, and intellectual strength. On the third day, guests begin to arrive. The ceremonies continue, and by the fourth day the young girl has been ushered into womanhood.

Today, although many reservation schools accept the absence of the junior high girls who undergo Kinaaldá, parents and family members cannot always be excused from work to hold such a four-day ceremony. Often, it must be postponed, and an abbreviated version takes place at a time when relatives can gather more readily.

Just as the timing of ceremonies can conflict with the demands of wage labor, other behaviors required of participants also present a problem. During a funeral period, family members of the deceased cannot bathe until the formal cleansing held at the end of the four-day ceremony. Other ceremonies also conclude this way. Bathing constraints were tolerable when the family stayed together at the ceremonial site. But for people whose livelihood is away from the enclave, especially those in the service industries, unwashed hair can be unpleasant and unacceptable. During the summer, it became difficult for Navajos working at the monument.

"I can't wait to take a shower," moaned one of bookstore clerks at the visitor center. She was in mourning for a relative but had to be at work, where she interacted closely with visitors. "I know what you mean," Margarita responded. "My hair gets so dirty, and the rest of me as well. So I try to get close to the fire. Then I smell like smoke instead of sweat."

There are other areas in which wage labor and Navajo daily life conflict. For instance, private telephone service on the reservation is still limited; it is a costly innovation and not a spending priority in most households. People use the public phones located in "towns" that are little more than extensions of nineteenth-century trading posts. Today, they center on a convenience store, gas station, laundromat, and video rental service—plywood and metal additions to the original log-beamed trader's headquarters. Phoning in sick to work can mean a thirty-mile trip on unpaved roads to reach the only phone in the area. Such an expedition requires a ride, a passable road, and a working telephone.

On the day after Easter, Charlie and I hiked down the Tunnel Trail past Sleeping Duck Ruin. The warm spring weather had been a boon for the Navajo guides, who earned eight dollars an hour taking tourists into the canyon on foot or in four-wheel-drive vehicles belonging to the visitors. For the past several days, they had been hiking only—half-day and all-day treks on the many winding trails. In spite of the Easter holiday, the canyon was closed to vehicle traffic all week. The high, fast waters from the snowmelt in the Chuska Mountains had filled the wash with swirling torrents and turned the bottom into lethal quicksand.

After much discussion, the Park Service decided to reopen the wash, provided that vehicles traveled in pairs for safety. Tourists at the visitor center grumbled at being asked to wait for a second vehicle to arrive, and rangers explained patiently that it was for their own protection. At about half past ten, the first two vehicles entered the canyon.

As Charlie and I moved from the Tunnel Trail toward the wash, we heard the sound of an engine and several shouting voices. A green Chevy Blazer was mired in mud up past its hubcaps. Two guides—Margarita's cousin, Jeremiah Tso, and Mark Jimmy—were soaked to the waist, eyeing the situation with the skill that comes from having dealt with this folly often. Jeremiah had the jack, and Mark was putting logs and boards under the wheels to provide traction. The driver of the truck, a middle-aged Coloradoan with graying hair, was skeptical but willing to help. A few hundred feet behind, the four-wheel-drive Toyota belonging to the second group of visitors idled patiently. Once they got the Blazer moving, the guides would stake out the safest route through the thick, pink, roiling soup of the wash.

Through all this, a woman passenger sat, unsmiling, in the Blazer. Dressed in a button-down blue shirt and L. L. Bean shorts, she fiddled with her camera, torn between getting out to take a picture of the adventure and staying dry in the front seat. The two guides joked merrily in Navajo. Charlie and I were already there, and the driver of the Toyota waded in to add his weight to ours. The wheels spun and dug, and smelled like burning rubber.

"Do you need my weight?" Charlie asked suddenly, as the guides tried to jack up the front of the car. "I want this picture. It'll illustrate leverage for a physics textbook I'm working on!" They looked at Charlie as if he were crazy. The woman in the Blazer seemed to sense that this was fun, but was unsure if it was safe and reluctant to get out to take a picture. "It's cold," I said, "but it feels neat." She opened the door, which was still above the waterline, and took off one of her Timberland boots. One toe tested the water but returned quickly to the car. Behind us, some canyon wrens trilled their descending song while Jeremiah forced another length of board under the front tire. Mark walked back from where he had marked a course through the wash with slender willow poles.

"Okay," said Jeremiah, turning to the driver. "You get back into the car. Everybody else push. When you start moving, navigate between the poles." He turned to the second driver. "Then you get back into the Toyota, and follow—fast!"

We gave one last massive shove, and the Blazer started to move. I jumped away quickly and fell backward into the wash, laughing. The two vehicles roared into the shallows ahead, and Jeremiah and Mark ran after them, each jumping into one of the cars. As they sped up-canyon, water and sand flying beside them, Raven swooped low over the wash.

"Ah-ah-ah-ah-ah," she cried, as she caught a breeze and lifted easily back up into the sky. She seemed to be laughing at us poor, foolish humans, forced to travel in such an inferior fashion.

I got to know Jeremiah better during that visit. He loved to hike and explore, and I enjoyed seeing new parts of the canyon. During long meanders together, we shared stories about our families and our lives. His wife, Caroline, was a weaver who worked as a seasonal ranger. They had three children—two boys and a teenaged girl—who, he told me, longed for a bedroom set and privacy amidst the open-door bustle of the Navajo family.

Meditation at Canyon de Chelly.

One morning, Jeremiah and I walked out behind Chinle, up onto the long plain that looks back toward the canyon. We talked of his struggle with alcohol and about how we, as humans, knew what we believed to be true. As I became more comfortable with my Navajo friends, many of our conversations turned to philosophy and religion.

I was raised Catholic but drifted away from formal religious practice as a young adult. In the last few years, though, I had become religious in a different way. I moved to a ninety-acre farm and was acutely aware of the natural cycles of life—the lengthening or shortening of the days, the return of wild animals in springtime, the need to prepare for winter long in advance of the first snows. The cycles were more than time marked on a calendar for me. I knew the passage of the seasons because I had become part of them.

Jeremiah was raised in the canyon with the knowledge of the Holy Ones in the places where these sacred beings walked and set out the Navajo Way. The cycles that I was just learning to feel were those he grew up with. For his part, he was now exploring the evangelical Christian church in an attempt to put some meaning into the way life was changing around him.

We walked through the red sand and across some fine rock on Kit Carson Mesa to a curved window of stone. A large arch narrowed to slender capstone; if you stood to one side, there was a pristine view. Move a few inches to the right, however, and the massive towers of the power company peered through, the steel *ye'ii'bichei*—gods—of progress and uncertainty. I wondered about Jeremiah. How was he cut off from the holiness of the canyon? Why was he asking for guidance from the Christian god, while I asked wisdom from the spirits of nature?

Beyond the arch was a small canyon, a narrow flow place of seasonal torrents. As we walked toward it, we talked about peace and being out of harmony, and of the different ways to worship. I told him a little about my mother's illness and how helpless I felt as the woman I had known slipped away from me.

"What do you do when you feel like that?" Jeremiah asked. "Sometimes I drink. Sometimes I try to meditate." "How do you meditate?" he asked. "Not very well, really. I close my eyes, and think about one thing—an eagle flying into the sun, maybe. Mostly I just try to sit still." Jeremiah sat down on a rock and looked into the distance. "Let's try it. First I'll say a prayer in Navajo, one that is my special prayer, and you think about your mother. Then we can meditate."

I looked at him curiously. "How much of what you tell me can I repeat, Jeremiah?" I asked. "How much can I write about?" I was thinking about a hike we had taken a few days earlier, when we climbed to the back side of Spider Rock and Jeremiah told me the story of how Spider Woman taught the people to weave.

Jeremiah laughed. "I won't say anything you can't repeat. Besides, I never tell you the whole story. I always leave out a few pieces. We always do. Navajos have been telling anthropologists only part of the story for the last hundred years." He looked at me out of the corner of his eye to gauge my reaction, and switched to Navajo. His deep voice echoed across the canyon as we sat together in the morning light.

Chapter 3

Warm Golden Wind

"It's hot and it's dry and it's dusty, and we're gonna go to Colorado in the morning," a teenaged girl whined into one of the two pay telephones outside the Thunderbird Lodge. Tugging on her Grand Canyon Day-Glo T-shirt, she added, "I don't want to be here, Dad."

The prevailing mood of the tourists waiting in line to use the phones wasn't hard to assess. It was early July and the rains had not yet come. A constant blast of hot, sharp sand whipped into the air in the lower canyon; for those not touched by de Chelly's beauty, hiking could be a trial.

Charlie and I, along with Charlie's fiancée, Marty, had returned to the canyon in 1991 to spend most of the summer. We set up tents in the Cottonwood Campground. Though the monument was short staffed, housing for volunteers was still at a premium. Even Margarita could not be accommodated in the Park Service duplexes, and she and her daughter, Carla, often shared my ten-by-ten tent.

The campground was filled with RVers and tenters from across the country as well as Germany, Italy, and France. Some stayed for up to a week, returning each evening from long hikes exhausted and delighted. Others, disappointed they couldn't enter the canyon at will, were anxious to move on.

The Park Service began the day early for the visitors, serving hot, strong coffee at the fire circle in the campground amphitheater. Since I was scheduled to lead a half-day hike, I woke at dawn and joined ranger Caroline Tso. There were about ten people—visitors, rangers, and guides—sitting around the fire, clutching their mugs of coffee. "That cowboy coffee?" asked a Californian, eyeing the huge, fire-smudged, black-and-white enamel coffeepot that rested precariously on a nest of sweet-smelling juniper logs. Caroline smiled. "We don't make cowboy coffee around here," she told the visitor. "We're Indians." Everybody laughed.

55

She had started the fire with just one match and some wadded-up newspapers. A New Yorker in the group murmured in amazed approval; where he came from, firewood was perpetually damp. "Can I ask you a question?" asked one of the other visitors, taking her cue from Caroline's easy humor. "I wondered about the round houses we saw out behind the regular houses. Do people live in those?" Caroline gave a quick history of the hogan. Other questions, about Navajo schools, religion, and daily life, followed.

At eight o'clock, I walked over the hill to Park Service headquarters with a few of the visitors to begin the four-hour morning hike through the canyon bottom. The day's group included children and seniors, a seventy-year gap dividing the youngest from the oldest. They came clad in baseball caps and cameras, blue jeans or deep-pocketed shorts, soft-sided hiking shoes or sneakers. The walking would be arduous, through beach-like sand to magnificent panels of pictographs and petroglyphs, past thousand-year-old ruins, and through gaily prancing flocks of sheep and goats.

As interpretive rangers, we took turns leading the hikes, and each of us did it a little differently. I was the anthropologist, focusing on canyon prehistory and contemporary culture. Margarita described growing up in the canyon, sharing stories of her childhood. Chad Benally loved to show visitors how to do rock art and make arrowheads, and Caroline talked about weaving, sandpainting, and other Navajo crafts.

On the Tunnel Trail, visitors were surrounded by the geological and ethnobotanical tale of the canyon. It continued down stone and log steps, past the perfect white blossoms of the datura plant, into wide pastures at the bottom. Angora goats grazed in bucolic disarray, tempting the hikers to reach for their cameras. I launched into a parable of caution.

"When you walk in the canyon, you are walking through Navajo backyards," I told them. "Imagine that you are mowing the lawn in front of your house when a busload of visitors from Papua, New Guinea, pulls up. They've never seen this quaint custom before. Are you gathering food? Will you build with the grass? Is it ceremonial behavior? They all pull out cameras and start shooting pictures. Now, the first day it might be humorous, and the second, tolerable, but pretty soon it would become old and you'd be tired of smiling for the cameras." The visitors thought about it; most nodded in understanding and went back to photographing ruins.

We moved out of the thick growth of tamarisk and Russian olive into the shifting sand of the wash. The sun was burning from a cloudless sky whose blue was almost palpable. From around the bend of Sleeping Duck Rock the smell of gasoline mixed with a grinding, rumbling noise, and one of the mint-green, twelve-wheeled Thunderbird Lodge tour trucks appeared. Carrying twenty-four passengers each, they provided half-day and full-day tours for those who would rather not walk.

"There goes the 'shake-and-bake,'" I told the hikers. With a slight sense of superiority, the group waved to the truck and its driver. White-haired ladies gave a gracious response, holding wide-brimmed hats with one hand and waving with the other. "If that's the shake-and-bake, what are we?" a young boy asked me. I paused for a moment. "The 'walk-and-talk,'" I replied.

Suddenly, the whinny of a horse startled us from behind. A Navajo guide and three visitors, all on horseback, emerged from a curtain of cottonwoods along the cliff wall. The boy stood watching as the horses munched at grass and then galloped across the wash. "Well then," he said in a satisfied tone, "those guys must be the 'clop-and-plop'!"

The number of visitors to the canyon has risen steadily in recent years. More than 1,000 people pass through the visitor center each day during the peak of the summer season. The typical visitor spends less than a day and experiences the canyon only from rim-drive overlooks. Interaction with Navajo residents is minimal. In fact, many visitors are unaware that the canyon is occupied, or expect to find a living museum of the last century in Navajo daily life. Rangers face the task of providing culturally sensitive material to people who are either ill informed or misinformed about contemporary Navajo life in the canyon.

The Park Service has increased the number of Navajo interpreters in an effort to provide a Navajo perspective. On summer evenings, ranger-led programs on history, prehistory, ecology, and current issues are offered. Those that concern Navajo culture and history are designed for a Navajo audience, and a growing number of Native Americans from Arizona and New Mexico are visiting the canyon. For non-Navajo visitors, the programs provide a window into the lives and practices of the residents.

Like the daytime hikes, the evening programs express the individual ranger's particular interests. In one program, Margarita described the significance of the Navajo hair bun and cradleboard. For the Columbus Quincentennial she collected oral histories that recounted the experiences of families whose members have not forgotten the coming of the Spanish and the Anglos into the region. Chad told the story of the hogan, using slides and poetry. Another Navajo ranger demonstrated the process of rug making from "sheep to rug"—shearing an Angora goat and then carding, spinning, and weaving the wool.

All local motels and the Cottonwood Campground fill to capacity between Memorial Day and Labor Day. Entrance to the canyon is permitted only on ranger-led hikes or with authorized Navajo guides. Many visitors choose half-day and full-day motor excursions run by the Thunderbird Lodge, a non-Navajo concession that employs a number of Navajo drivers and guides.

The Park Service is considering limiting the Thunderbird tours to half-day excursions that would go only partway up the two canyons. The big trucks are both intrusive and destructive, contributing to serious erosion in the bed of the wash. A back-country management plan supports guided visits on foot and horseback. For the interpreters, sharing tradition with the public can also be a learning experience, an interchange of ideas and values that is most apt to occur during longer visits. The Navajo-run Tsegi Guide Association, working in conjunction with the Park Service, trains and authorizes residents to guide visitors into the canyon.

The only trail accessible to visitors without a guide is the walk to the White House Ruin. This two-and-a-half-mile round-trip takes hikers past some of the best examples of the area's geology. At the bottom is the White House, a fenced, partially stabilized ruin that was seriously damaged by floods and erosion during the early decades of the last century. Some visitors, disappointed to find they cannot enter the ruin, continue on to Mesa Verde in Colorado, where they can walk through the rebuilt structures of the Anasazi past. Others are more accepting of the Park Service mandate to "preserve and protect," which means limited public access to fragile sites and structures.

Thunderbird Lodge tour trucks at White House Ruin.

The summer continued dry and hot, but the rains finally came on a warm afternoon in mid July. As Charlie and I walked down the slope to Twin Trails Canyon, the wind bent the corn to the west, its dark-green foliage set off against the chartreuse, filigreed stems of the rabbitbrush. Gray-and-black potsherds and red plastic lay together in the sandy soil.

Looking down, I noticed the back end of a thick, white chert projectile point that had washed out in the center of the well-used trail. A short distance away, pink, red, salmon, maroon, gray, ochre, and white flakes of rock—chipping debris washed together by past rains—clustered in a crevice. Large cores and smaller chips graced a stony knoll overlooking the fertile fields of this valley's wide side canyon. How do you "preserve and protect" in an area still in use, I wondered.

In the distance, Chinle was veiled in the dry rains known as virgas, showers that evaporate in the summer heat before reaching the ground. Ahead, across the slick rock and past a gaping arroyo, the Archaeology Camp sat sheltered in a broad cottonwood grove that divided two active farms. This part of Canyon del Muerto was perhaps the widest circle of arable land in the area, the corn dwarfing anything found across the peninsula in de Chelly. In the midst of the fields, gray-green tents housed crews of Park Service employees and students from Northern Arizona University who were working to survey, document, map, and determine the stability of the canyon's ruins—both those already charted and those not previously mapped. The cluster looked like a military encampment, almost a vision of Kit Carson's invading troops 130 years ago.

Charlie and I continued up the canyon past the empty "arch' camp" and joined Margarita at Big Cave. An archaeological contingent was working there as well, drawing and measuring in a massive overhang that once held a multitude of Basketmaker and Anasazi structures. The alcove was highly eroded, and many of the occupational areas had been washed away by the waterfalls that poured over the rim each year during the monsoon-like July rains.

As we approached the site, Margarita and I talked about archaeology and its purpose. The last real excavation in the canyon had taken place in the 1970s at Antelope House. Margarita and Drew Chambers, the director of the Park Service project at Big Cave, tried to explain to the canyon residents this resumption of archaeological activity after such a long interval. "What more do they want here?" many of the residents had asked Margarita. "Didn't they dig it all up a long time ago and take it away? They come in and do what they have to do, and then we don't hear anything more from them."

Margarita and Drew agreed that dialogue with the residents was key to working out the delicate problem of preservation and protection of extensive prehistoric and historic remains in a residential area. These people were no longer merely mute observers of the work going on around them. They wanted to know what was happening, how it would affect them and their use of land, and who would benefit. As a canyon resident herself, Margarita tried to convey to the Park Service the Navajo feeling about the sacred character of certain locations. As a representative of the Park Service, she attempted to show canyon residents that Park Service knowledge about these sites might save them from destruction.

As we looked up at the quiet concentration of work in the overhang, Margarita told me that working for both the Park Service and the residents was a cultural balancing act. "I feel like I've been handed a big pot of beans and don't know if I'll get through this without spilling it," she remarked. "We could hold town meetings in the chapter houses and use KTNN to get the word out," she went on. The chapter houses were community centers, gathering places for meetings and social occasions. "You think people would come?" I asked. We both remembered the briefing held for Navajo residents the previous summer at the end of the first archaeological season. Its sparse attendance was testimony to the difficult task of getting people to come to a specific location at a set time. "You'd have to make sure there weren't any ceremonies going on that weekend," Margarita said. I laughed. "That's a losing proposition in the summer." "It is," Margarita agreed. "I told Drew: For this to work, we have to take the news to the people."

We continued climbing, carefully, and reached the edge of the site. I wasn't sure which way to move, afraid of what the Vibram soles of my hiking boots might crush. Walls fallen from three-story structures lay underfoot all around. We passed a layered lattice of collapsed roofs on our left as we started into the overhang.

The chief archaeologist's voice echoed through the huge space as he instructed several people taking measurements along the west side of the cave. Two others were using a soil color chart to key dusky-red-and-cream pictographs. "Eight-two white," called a young worker to her companion as they recorded coded colors on drawings done on graph paper.

"If this place hadn't been excavated back in the '30s it would be in better shape today," commented Dave Breternitz, a venerable Southwestern archaeologist working with the project for the summer. "There's no excuse for it. Those guys just looted the site and left. Then the goats came in and filled in the open areas. It's an *après*-excavation nightmare."

At one end of the overhang, an ax-hewn beam more than 1,000 years old supported a line of Basketmaker-era stone slabs. Some distance away was the remains of a great kiva. The scrutiny of mapping turned up a small ceramic deer's head and a cache of stained and matted yucca pads that answered a basic question about feminine hygiene; I often wondered what Basketmaker women used as menstrual pads.

The acoustics in the overhang were like a sophisticated amplification system. Even when people talked in hushed tones, anything that was said on one side was audible on the other. I tried to imagine the din of hundreds of occupants.

We returned to the camp at dusk, and Margarita headed back to Park Service headquarters on a four-wheeled "quad runner." Charlie and I went down-canyon a few hundred feet to talk with Dan Foley, a Navajo farmer who was also a pharmacist with the Public Health Service in Chinle. He grew corn and alfalfa on family land, getting three cuttings a year from the alfalfa. The land had extensive irrigation ditches, all in need of repair.

"I'm a weekend farmer," Dan told us. His whole family came in from Chinle on weekends, the kids playing next to the arch' camp while the adults tended the farm and shoveled out the irrigation ditches.

Dan grew up at Twin Trails, where his father made the family's boots and worked the land with the horse-drawn equipment that was still in evidence. For the past several months, he had met with the Park Service as a representative of the residents while the monument's administrators finished writing their back-country management plan. "The archaeologists are okay," he said. "They're using new methods, not just digging. But sometimes I have to wait for their clearances when I want to make improvements on my land, like putting in that new irrigation channel."

Dappled gray clouds obscured the sun the next morning. After breakfast, we loaded into the pickup and drove a few miles down-canyon to begin the day's reconnaissance. The archaeological survey was moving more slowly than had been planned because there was more to document than previous work had indicated. The sites were located high on the canyon walls in areas that seemed virtually inaccessible except for the evidence of centuries of human and animal traffic.

For this kind of work, one needed good knees, great lungs, and a sense of adventure. The crew scrambled up the talus to investigate two possible shelters, and the most fearless member headed for the highest alcove. After ten minutes, he called back down, pronouncing the alcove devoid of cultural material. In the lower shelter, five hundred feet above the canyon floor, the documentation process began. A few Navajo and prehistoric potsherds, a shell pendant, a lens of charcoal, mealing bins, some cord, and crude rock art defined a site of indeterminate age. Sheep had been there, as in most locations, and Navajo users had left a bucket and a tin cup. One painted sherd triggered an animated discussion of pottery types in this laboratory of learning along the sandstone wall.

Back down the talus rubble, back up another slope, higher still and more precipitous. This time there were whoops and cries of excitement. It was a Basketmaker site, left virtually untouched, comprising five storage

areas and twenty sealed cysts. The site had been dug down to the hardpan in the worst possible location—a northern aspect, on a ten- to fifteen-foot ledge that plunged straight down. The joy of discovery was tempered by the knowledge that there was so much more to be found. Listening to Drew's exhilarated descriptions, I remembered something Margarita said the previous winter: "If we hadn't had taboos about entering these places, they wouldn't be preserved for you to document now."

The philosophy that guides contemporary archaeology at Canyon de Chelly and elsewhere is one of preserving the landscape while documenting the existence and condition of ruins and sacred sites. The large-scale excavations of the past have been minimized. The current objective is to find the sites, record their condition, and try to keep them from deteriorating further.

In a region where prehistoric and historic land use has left behind an extensive legacy of artifacts and other cultural remains, farming and road construction often turn up significant materials. One purpose of archaeological and ethnographic surveys is to identify these areas before construction or land development takes place, thereby avoiding the conflict and delay that usually result from salvage archaeology, in which construction is halted while archaeological materials are collected.

The Navajos remember the looting that characterized archaeological activity at Canyon de Chelly during the first half of the last century. They are concerned that the identification of further sites may result in more land being placed off-limits to them. It is the job of ethnoarchaeologists to explain to residents the "wait-and-see" techniques that are a part of current practice, a philosophy that anticipates technological advances that will make obsolete the destruction of sites through digging.

As a comprehensive program of conservation and preservation of prehistoric and historic remains, cultural resource management involves more than simply cataloguing and analyzing artifacts and structures. Throughout the Southwest, cultural resources include land considered sacred by native peoples. Places where people go to gather plants, offer prayers, and hold ceremonies have a special significance. Often such locations are known only to *hataalii*—medicine men—or other elders. A challenge facing land developers and archaeologists is to identify these places and avoid potential conflict by rerouting roads and revising other projects.

Canyon de Chelly has long been a place of sacred significance to the people who live there. In some instances, knowledge about a site is held exclusively by members of one family; other locations are utilized by a great number of people. The canyon is a spiritual home to people whose

Previous page: Canyon del Muerto near Twin Trails.

oral traditions and practices link them to the land and sky and all living things. Honoring these relationships involves the Park Service in a delicate balance: to preserve the land for the physical and spiritual needs of the residents, to preserve archaeological remains for the future, and to sponsor tourism in a responsible and sustainable fashion.

Due to a resurgence of interest in pre-Christian, nature-based religious philosophies, canyon rangers and residents alike have had to contend with visitors searching for spiritual meaning. The Park Service's attitude toward those who might seek to appropriate Navajo sacred sites and practices into their lives is gently discouraging:

> "The specific beliefs, sites, ceremonies, work for the Navajo people because of the strong depth of their culture and traditions," the monument's chief interpretive ranger, Wilson Hunter, wrote in the canyon newspaper in 1991. "Most non-Navajo visitors were not raised in Navajo traditions. These places and events cannot have the same meaning, but there are lessons of value here for all visitors. . . . You can find a place that has special meaning for you and it can be your special place. . . . It is the idea, the feeling you carry with you, which makes any place sacred. . . . By listening to the canyon and putting ourselves in contact with the people here, perhaps we can come to a better understanding of just where 'home' is for all of us. By traveling to Canyon de Chelly we may be able to add more meaning to the place we call 'home' when we return there."

On a hot, still morning, Charlie and I hiked down into de Chelly canyon along the twisting switchbacks of White Sands Trail. We were on our way to visit Harry Etcitty, a longtime canyon guide, on his land near Sliding House. The long-awaited rains had swelled Chinle Wash and given life to an infinite number of small, biting creatures: mosquitoes, gnats, and flies. The worst of these were the deerflies. If one was foolish enough to hike this section of the canyon in shorts, they gladly hitched a ride, hanging on to the backs of legs with bloodthirsty jaws.

Insects thrive in the dense undergrowth of cottonwood, tamarisk, and Russian olive, which traps moisture and provides excellent breeding grounds. A legacy of the early days of Park Service tenure in the canyon, the trees had been introduced in an effort to control continuing erosion, the product of drought and purported overgrazing. We were curious about that era and about the agreements that allowed a national monument to be established on Navajo land. It seemed likely that Harry Etcitty would have some recollections of events of the 1930s.

Harry had been born and raised in the canyon and was one of many locals who worked for Earl Morris at the excavations at Mummy Cave. Although he was just a schoolboy at the time, Harry had a good command of English—a rare skill in those days—and served as a translator for the expedition. Later, he participated in digs at Aztec Ruin, Chaco Canyon, and Mesa Verde.

Harry was one of the few Navajo "elderlies" who still tried to maintain the seasonal round of canyon life by relocating his goats and sheep from winter residences on the rim to peninsula sheep camp in early spring, and then down to the canyon bottom for the heat of summer. The constant movement of the livestock allowed the pasture to regenerate, and traditionally the entire family moved with the herd. The Etcitty family appeared in a widely circulated documentary film called *Seasons of the Navajo*, which added to Harry's fame as a knowledgeable guide. He continued to herd sheep and to take visitors through the canyon in their four-wheel-drive vehicles.

When Charlie and I arrived, Harry was sitting at a well-worn table in the shade of ancient cottonwoods in front of his large, sturdy hogan. The land was close to the canyon wall, and the towering cliffs protected shoulder-high corn that looked healthy though in need of weeding. Except for the bleating of goats and sheep, and the dogs rustling in the dry cottonwood leaves on the ground, the farm was curiously still and silent without the sound of children. There were no grandchildren darting between the wandering stock, no young voices calling out gaily in Navajo.

"Going to the sheep dip?" Charlie asked Harry, referring to the practice of disinfecting the herds that took place each summer throughout the reservation. (Sheep dips have since been banned because of the damage caused by the potent chemicals.) The Etcittys had a place near Black Rock up on the peninsula, and the dip was scheduled for the following Sunday. "Nope," answered Harry. "Can't get there."

He looked at us with steady, penetrating eyes, in violation of the Navajo tenet that it is impolite to look someone directly in the eye. Perhaps different rules applied with white folks, I thought. "Grandkids usually here to help me get these sheep up that Black Rock Trail," Harry added, "but they're not here this summer." "How come?" I asked. The flies buzzed through his long silence. He smiled knowingly, and his answer came in two words. "Chinle TV."

Harry pushed his chair back from the table and walked with care toward the hogan. He moved slowly, the eighty-two years spent herding and walking this canyon beginning to show. I could hear him shuffling papers inside. Then he returned with two carefully preserved black-and-white photos. The first showed a serious, very handsome youth, his dark hair cut above the ears. It was Harry as a young marine, fifty years ago. One couldn't miss the eyes. The second photo was of a young woman, vibrant and beautiful, her hair pulled back in a traditional bun, the velveteen shirt adorned with silver and turquoise necklaces. "That's my wife," Harry said, extending his lower lip to point at the photo. "She's seventy-six. She's getting old."

Harry Etcitty, longtime canyon guide.

I had seen Harry's wife in *Seasons*, watched her weave and cook and shear the sheep, and hoped someday I could be that kind of old. Harry stared at me, almost flirtatiously, waiting for comment. I took the opportunity to ask him about the origins of the canyon's monument status.

Harry thought about it. "I was living over in del Muerto side back then—that's where I was born—when word started coming down that the government was going to put a fence around the whole canyon. We were worried, because we used those trails to take the stock in and out, and we were afraid we couldn't get them through the fences. When the government came they said there'd be lots of jobs planting trees and trying to control erosion, and we thought that would be good. But that only lasted about two summers and one winter. Then everybody just went back to herding sheep."

Harry, Charlie, and I shared a lunch of tuna fish and ripe cantaloupe. Harry took the melon seeds and laid them on a tree stump to dry, hoping that they would produce fruit for him the following year. We promised to return in the next months with the photos Charlie had taken.

As we walked back through the wash, we startled a group of horses drinking in the shallow flow. Some belonged to Harry, others to relatives living farther down the trail. Many of the women and children were at their peninsula homes, where higher altitudes and additional moisture provided pasture in the late summer. As September approached, part of the family would move back to the rim or to their government housing in town, to be closer to the school busses at the start of the term.

Those who continue to farm and keep livestock at Canyon de Chelly face some of the same concerns as family farmers throughout the nation. How do you take a way of life that is bound up in a basic relationship with the land and environment around you, and make it provide support for your family? Each spring landholders bring aging tractors into the canyon to prepare the fields for planting. On the de Chelly, or south, side, the fields are devoted almost exclusively to corn and squash, and are dependent on rainfall and runoff for survival through the summer. North-side agriculture is more ambitious—alfalfa hay supplements the corn crop, and the tyranny of rain and machinery affects the success or failure of each season's three to four cuttings.

Following the establishment of the national monument in the mid-1930s, government-funded conservation efforts sponsored widespread tree planting and flood control projects. Dams were constructed from Tsaile Lake to the Twin Trails area of Canyon del Muerto, allowing the impounded waters of the lake to be released periodically to feed irrigation systems along the way. This series of low-tech dams was relatively successful in bringing water to the fields during dry periods.

Back-country management proposals include the construction of new water control areas, and residents are eager to increase the size of irrigation systems to bring additional acreage into production. Continued dialogue must take place between the Park Service and canyon residents, since each new plow furrow inevitably uncovers archaeological remains. Also at issue is the question of grazing management. Fenced fields keep livestock away from crops, but they also limit the movement of animals and contribute to continuing erosion along the banks of the wash.

Most canyon visitors are unaware of these issues. They come here to look at the ruins, photograph the magic, and see the Indians, not to ponder the questions of survival that confront the canyon and the rest of the reservation.

A group of tourists in color-coordinated outfits gathered around Caroline Tso at sunset at the junction overlook. They stood behind a stand of piñon and juniper, seeking shelter from the persistent wind that whipped across the canyon and sent Caroline's broad-brimmed Smoky hat skittering away.

Caroline was demonstrating sandpainting, using a large rubber basin to keep the multicolored grains from scattering to the wind. The basin was filled with a base of red canyon sand, and Caroline worked quickly and accurately with the four sacred colors: white, deep red ochre, yellow ochre, and black. The colors were all naturally occurring pigments, ground in an abalone shell from nuggets found in the area surrounding Canyon de Chelly. Often they were unexpected gifts, brought back by Caroline's husband, Jeremiah, from one of his guided hikes, or collected by friends who knew that this was one of Caroline's special interests.

"Was sandpainting combined with herb medicines?" asked a young woman. "Yes," Caroline answered, closing her hand around a trickle of sand that had just become a corn stalk. "Herb drinking, singing, sweat baths, ceremonies lasting one to nine nights. Want to try?" Several children came forward eagerly.

"Does it matter which hand you use?" asked a ten-year-old boy, picking up black sand in earnest concentration. "If you're left-handed, use your left hand." Caroline told him. The grains began to drop, first in hesitant splotches, then evenly, one grain at a time. "Hey, you're doing it wrong!" yelled his sister over the noise of the wind. Her brother simply ignored her as he tried to emulate Navajo sacred art.

Earlier that day, Caroline demonstrated flint-knapping—the art of making arrowheads out of stone that she and Jeremiah learned from older relatives. Though she worked full-time in the summers, in her off hours Caroline returned home to weave large, intricate rugs—all artistic masterpieces. Differing somewhat from classic Navajo designs, they incorporated the complicated patterns of a Persian rug in rich colors and textures that brought high prices from those who special-ordered the pieces. In her mid-thirties, Caroline was proof that the craft was not left to the grandmothers.

Like Caroline, Margarita's cousin, Linda, was also a weaver, the widowed mother of three young children. They lived in what was referred to as the "solar housing" at Tsaile but spent as much time as possible at the winter and summer camps, where the kids could herd sheep, ride horses, and keep themselves occupied with outdoor activities.

"My grandma got up before dawn to pray the sun into the new day. I get up before dawn to have a few hours to weave before the kids wake up. I'll breathe a sigh of relief when the last of the kids goes to Head Start in the fall!" Linda said. "Then I'll have hours of uninterrupted time to work. I can finish a rug in about three weeks, working steady." She bent behind the large standing loom in her kitchen to tie off a color and bring in a new piece of yarn on the chief's blanket, her current project.

Like many weavers, Linda bought her wool commercially, saving the hours of labor involved in shearing, washing, carding, spinning, and dyeing wool from one's own sheep. Although commercial yarns provide a wider range of colors and result in a less coarse rug, the colors of the non-

Linda weaves at home.

commercial fibers have a special quality, a beauty produced by natural dyes and the lanolin smell that never completely leaves the wool. As fewer and fewer weavers prepare their own wool, that quality is becoming a part of history, like so many other facets of Navajo daily life.

"Will you be working on Thursday, Jeanne?" Margarita asked me one day in the visitor center. We were both in uniform, she in full dress grays, and I in the khaki and green of the volunteer.

"I'm off Thursday and Friday. Why?"

"Do you think you'd have the time to take my mom and stepdad and a couple of others to Gallup to shop for the Squaw Dance?"

I smiled to myself, secretly delighted. It was 1992, my third summer at Canyon de Chelly. I returned again as a volunteer for a month and reserved the usual subcompact economy car, specifically requesting a hatchback. But when I presented myself at the airport rental agency desk, the clerk told me that only sedans were available. Would I take a seven-passenger minivan for the same price? It was a substitution made in heaven. The huge, maroon luxury vehicle was clearly designed to take extended families, wandering students, and stranded visitors shopping in far-off places. I couldn't wait to fill it with Margarita's family, slip a flute tape by her cousin, Navajo-Ute musician R. Carlos Nakai, into the stereo, and just cruise.

The ceremony known as the Squaw Dance, or Enemy Way, was held for someone who was deemed to be out of harmony because of contact with non-Navajo forces or individuals. A combination healing, religious, and social event, it lasted five days and took as many weeks of advance preparation. It required the services of a singer trained in the ceremony as well as a considerable financial outlay for food and shelter for scores of participants. This particular Enemy Way was for one of Margarita's cousins who just returned from military service. The family had been sewing and weaving ceremonial clothing and blankets, and cooking for days, and had already hosted a preceremony gathering at which family and clan members contributed to the cost of the event.

When Margarita asked me to attend as a friend of the family, I was honored but confused. I knew that contact with biligáanas was one of the common causes of disharmony, and I felt uncomfortable attending a ceremony designed to remedy such an affliction. "Are you sure you want me there?" I asked Margarita. "I talked to my cousin's family and they said it was okay. You're our guest," she replied.

It was just about noon on Thursday when I drove into Tsaile and picked up Margarita's sister, Lora; their mother, Karen; Karen's husband, Leonard; and Margarita's daughter, Carla, at the solar housing near Diné College. Moving to Tsaile had been a compromise for Karen and Leonard. Karen preferred to be in the canyon, but living there was becoming physically difficult for them. Leonard wanted to be closer to his own family in a nearby town. The Tsaile housing was near both the summer camp at Black Rock and the main road, and provided comforts the couple appreciated in their later years.

When I arrived, Lora, seven months pregnant, was resting on the couch. Karen was busy weaving a gray-and-red blanket, which she hoped to finish before the Squaw Dance as a gift for one of the participants. She sat in front of the loom, leaning on one hip with her legs to the left, cushioned by a huge pink teddy bear turned upside down. She was dressed in full-length, emerald-green satin, belted with a gray, red, green, and white woven sash, and wore all of her best turquoise and silver jewelry.

"Look at her," Lora said jokingly. "That's more jewelry than I've ever seen one Navajo grandma wear on a trip to Gallup." Leonard was dressed up too, and he looked healthy and clear-eyed after a long winter of illness. We all piled into the van and drove through the mountains, past Fort Defiance and Window Rock, toward Gallup. Lora and I were seated in front and talked about her pregnancy. She was on her own—the baby's father was in Denver—but she had the support of her family.

Lora explained a little more about the Squaw Dance. Among the items to be purchased in Gallup was velveteen, a gift for the young woman who would symbolize the female side of the unmarried male patient. We also needed to get Cracker Jacks and candy to be thrown to the waiting guests at dawn. On the first night, everyone would go on horseback or in cars to a location selected by the healer, and it was his family who would feed the hundreds who attended. The following night a feast would be served by the patient's family on their land.

As we pulled into Gallup, Karen said that she was hungry for a Chinese all-you-can-eat lunch. They had been eating mutton daily as they fed those who came by the Black Rock enclave to help build the shade house for the Squaw Dance; lo mein and egg rolls sounded good to all. I stopped the van and we went in and filled our plates. I said I would pay.

"You don't have to do that," Lora told me. "I know, but I want to," I said. "How many times in my life will I get to take a Navajo family out for Chinese food?" We filled our plates again, agreeing that we needed to be well fed before an afternoon spent shopping at one of the largest Wal-Mart stores in the Southwest. In Navajo, it is called *ya'ahsh din da'hi*, which translates roughly as "place you go into and don't come out for a long time." We didn't.

I shopped with Lora and Karen, moving up and down the busy aisles, checking lists. Other dressed-up grandmothers passed, but none was a match for Karen. In the fabric section, we selected the right shade of wine-colored velveteen. After more wandering, we added yarn, cream rinse, and an outfit for Carla. Eventually, Leonard and I wound up waiting in front of an enormous Pepsi display. He spoke little English, but we communicated with rolled eyes and smiles, and for the first time I didn't feel uncomfortable with one of the older men. At last, finished at Wal-Mart, we moved on to the Buy-for-Less store to purchase Kool-Aid, the makings of Rice Krispies treats, and, of course, Cracker Jacks.

I remained baffled by the Cracker Jack phenomenon. During my first year in the canyon, I had been astonished by the huge displays at the front of Basha's, and I once saw a grandmother pull a package out of her purse as we sat across from each other in the waiting room at a dental clinic. As a reliable anthropologist, I puzzled over the underlying meaning and symbolism of Cracker Jacks' popularity. I asked everybody I could, secretly convinced that it was some special reverence for the sacred corn that made it an item of choice at a Squaw Dance. My friends were tolerant. "We just like 'em," they told me. "And they have a surprise inside."

The day of the ceremony dawned dry, a great relief to those planning to drive or ride horseback into the Chuska Mountains later that evening. Margarita and I went together in the van, carrying warm bedding to use during the night. We also brought skeins of yarn with which to decorate the antenna and grill of our "ride" and others. The long line of vehicles, each decorated with loops of brightly colored yarn, wound its way slowly into the mountains in the falling light. High ponderosa flanked the juniper and piñon as the dirt track climbed toward the ceremony site.

A huge crowd of people stood in a wide circle outside their vehicles, facing a fine log hogan. Since this was one of the few occasions when I had been told explicitly not to take photographs, I had to use my mind as a camera, capturing the scene in literary images with as much accuracy as possible. I took out my notebook and started writing.

The setting sun was balanced by a rising full moon as we waited. Suddenly, twenty mounted men cantered in from the west, their hair blowing in the wind, their horses draped in skeins of colored wool. The riders were dressed in black and turquoise, bright pink and silver—colors of another time. They dismounted, and the hataalii—the singer-healer—and his patient entered the ceremonial hogan. The smell of cedar and sage drifted on the thin line of smoke that rose from the building's center.

Outside, the men and women stood in separate groups and talked in low voices while the children darted back and forth between the horses, waiting for the signal they knew was soon to come. From within the hogan, the steady voice of the singer anchored the people to the earth, releasing the powers within. Against a pink-and-orange sunset, the singer emerged, dressed in his finest calicos and turquoise. The children, knowing that it was time, ran to claim the skeins of yarn off the horses and vehicles for their grandmothers and their mothers.

In the dark, chill night of the desert mountains, the older men gathered near a huge pyramid of thirty-foot ponderosa logs. Later that night it would become a bonfire, but now small individual fires were lighted as the men began to sing the repetitive rhythms of the Squaw Dance songs. Margarita and I greeted other family members seated by their vehicles and then filled our plates with mutton and salad from the communal feast. Inside the hogan, the healing continued, and relatives and clansfolk drifted in and out to be part of the blessing and to pay their respects to the patient.

Some of Margarita's cousins struggled to assemble a propane-fired portable barbecue next to my van. Lanterns illuminated the pile of screws and bolts and a lengthy sheet of contradictory directions. They hoped to have the grill up and running by midnight in order to sell hot dogs, hamburgers, and coffee to a crowd of dancers and well-wishers who would remain at the ceremony until morning. In the interim, Carla sold brownies and Rice Krispies treats while the crowd visited to the accompaniment of the drums and the singing.

The previous year, I learned that selling food was a common practice at Navajo ceremonies and gatherings. I was invited to Black Rock for a family meal and wanted to bring some food as a contribution. Recalling how much the kids liked dill pickles, I went to Basha's and bought a five-gallon jar. At Black Rock, I unscrewed the lid and was about to place the jar on the table when one of the kids ran over. "How much for the pick-les?" he asked me. I looked at him blankly. "Take one." "Aren't you sell-ing them?" he asked.

I shook my head. "Why would I sell them?" "People always sell pick-les. Always." "Well, tell everybody these are part of dinner," I answered, feeling a bit foolish.

The huge bonfire was touched off shortly after midnight. Flames shot into the air and heat warmed our skins. "I don't think that's really safe," said Margarita's aunt Noreen, backing up her blue pickup as she watched a line of brush catch fire. The singers had already retreated, driven from the circle by the heat and force of the blaze. When at last it died down to manageable proportions they returned to their posts and, arm-in-arm, the dancers began a slow circling motion that would continue until morning.

Carla danced all night while the singers kept up a steady stream of chantlike rhythms. Margarita and I slept fitfully in the back of the van until rising light and morning sounds brought us back out into the juni-per-smoke dawn. Clutching Styrofoam cups of bitter coffee, the guests gathered in front of the hogan, the children's excitement rising with each passing moment. Finally, the patient and his family emerged from within carrying Cracker Jacks and candy, snack cakes, and canned pop. At a sig-nal, they tossed these tokens to the waiting crowd, after which they dis-tributed finer gifts for those who had sponsored the healing. Arms filled, the guests began to leave, heading down the mountain to Black Rock to begin the second day of ceremony.

Knowledge of ceremonies or songs is held by only a few Navajo peo-ple. These are the individuals whose spiritual calling moves them to apprentice themselves to elders who teach them the long and intricate words and movements. Some ceremonies, like the Enemy Way and the winter Ye'ii'bichei, are known by a number of healers. Others are kept by a single family or individual, and can pass out of use and knowledge if no one receives the teachings. During my Park Service training, a medicine man voiced concern over the erosion of traditional knowledge among his people. "What will happen to my grandfather's song when he is no longer there to sing it?" he asked. "Who will know the special words, the Coyote Way, when he is no longer here?"

Although sings remain an integral part of the healing process for the older Navajos and are also a reaffirmation of life philosophy, most young people have grown away from these lengthy and complex procedures. Their days are physically and temporally distant from those of their elders and from the practices needed to maintain that way of life. It takes a com-mitment of both will and energy to keep up with the sweat baths and sing-ing, the gathered herbs and healing teas, the farming and crafts that were the underpinnings of their grandparents' daily round.

Margarita, Charlie, and I hiked in to Margarita's land at the junction on a hot morning in July 1991. Reluctant to carry our heavy packs, we hailed a Thunderbird Lodge tour truck and put Carla on it with all the gear and water.

Margarita had begun to expand her homestead, inching toward her dream of reestablishing a farm at the old location. We had come into the canyon to work, to squeeze into Margarita's days off as many of the tasks of building a home and farm as we could. The newly enlarged shade house sheltered a double bed on a frame of gray plastic milk crates. With their openings faced out, the crates could also be used for storage. It was an ingenious idea for a bed frame, one I copied in my own house when I returned to New York at the end of the summer. A few cabinets had been built by an uncle, and a small dome tent was pitched so that its door opened into the arbor. In front of the kitchen area, faced stone blocks from a dismantled hogan at Black Rock waited to be made into a cooking hearth.

We walked back toward the canyon wall, where apricot trees were laden with ripe fruit. Margarita climbed a tree and shook a limb so that the fruit dropped to where Carla and I waited with buckets. We ate greedily before taking the remainder of the sweet, juicy apricots back to the shade house to be split and placed to dry on plastic dish drainers.

Margarita was in a nostalgic mood. "When I was little there was an orchard of apricots and peaches, and the family would fill the wagon, taking the fruit out of the canyon to dry or sell. It was a happy time. I

Margarita and Carla in Junction Farm kitchen.

remember driving the horses past the irrigation system." She paused. "We still had irrigation then—it came from pools and springs where the canyon walls come together back there. We had so many apples, growing behind fields of corn and squash." Of the apple orchard, only two gnarled trees remained, and these were sorely in need of pruning. One solitary peach tree struggled to survive in the dry soil.

We began to dig out the old fire circle, shoveling the rich ash into boxes that we hauled to the deep furrows of a plowed field. The ash removed, we enlarged the pit and circled it with the heavy stone, facing the opening to the east. A red tailgate from an old Ford pickup, reflector still in place, became a shelf and grate across the pit for cooking. Once the grate was positioned, Margarita built a fire and we began to prepare supper by dropping a yellow-blossomed bundle of fresh-picked Navajo tea into boiling water.

The smell of the paint burning off the tailgate mingled with the rich odor of bread frying as we cooked the first meal in the new kitchen. It was a strange menu of canned foods, noodles, and the thick pads of a prickly pear roasted over the coals in the fire. Margarita was experimenting, reaching back into the apricot summers to remember exactly how her grandmother prepared the prickly pear. We pulled a charred pad out of the fire and turned it carefully. The center was soft, and I tried to peel off the burned skin the way I would with a roasted pepper. Margarita looked at me skeptically. "I think my grandmother did it different," she said with a laugh.

After dinner, Carla took Charlie and me into a small cave at the back of the property, where we found handprints, pictographs, and a "star ceiling" of charcoal crosses drawn by Navajos in the nineteenth century. The falling night was exquisite. A clear coral wrapper of light illuminated the irregular rectangle of the cave's entrance. The air was filled with swirling cottonwood tufts, like the sideways snow of a winter blizzard. We sat quietly until the light faded and the sun disappeared, then climbed back out. A canyon kitty, obviously pregnant, mewed in the shadows, her cries echoing off the dark mass of Dog Rock which loomed solid against the blue-black horizon.

Margarita, Charlie, and I vowed to greet the dawn as the grandmothers did, rising early enough to reach the peninsula rim before the light. Up Yei Trail we went, groping for sand-filled hand- and toe-holds while our legs screamed that they had not yet awakened. Charlie and I walked silently behind Margarita, who was dressed in blue warm-up pants and a red-and-white-checked shirt, her thick black hair pulled back from her face. At the top of the trail, she stopped to gaze down on her land as it drowsed in the dawn. There was the persistent cry of a rooster and the tinkling of a goat bell from over on the south rim.

"When I was little," Margarita said, "we went up this trail in the mornings to the goats who were corralled here, then climbed back down, all before breakfast. It seemed so natural."

The goat corral was a crisscross of old, twisted wood, a series of tossed boulders forming a natural pen close to the edge of the canyon. A storage area of flat, piled sandstone and upright slabs stood near the rim. Gray pottery sherds, Navajo-made, were scattered on the ground near an old hogan that stood silently, its door perfectly placed to look toward the dawn. Just beyond, a datura bloomed in the shaded light. Some members of Margarita's family were born in that hogan, when its roof beams were covered with mud mortar and the canyon wind was louder than the sound of the autos we could hear making their way along the south rim.

Sunlight peaked through a slit in the hogan. A few rays hit the berries of a juniper just outside, almost as blue as Margarita's warm-up pants. We walked down to the point above the farm from which gathered firewood was thrown to the canyon floor. A great deal of wood lay in the cut now, juniper splintered by the fall, one piece standing upright, embedded in the soil.

We came down from Yei separately. The day before, Charlie and I climbed to a ledge in a side canyon near the farm. In a crevice at the back, a baby's burial had eroded and was now visible. I had told Margarita about it.

"I checked on that burial," she said when she returned. "I don't like going near it, but I wanted to be sure everything was okay. I added some cover, and it made me think. I walked through some places where I haven't been in a long time, and I remembered my family and what we used to do each day."

Later that morning, with no sign of the needed July rain, Margarita and I headed toward the fruit trees to water and prune. We gave a few buckets to the young peach tree struggling to stay alive in the brittle, cracked soil and tried to remember the correct season to trim dangling branches. "When do you prune?" I yelled back to Charlie, who had remained in the shade house. "Any time you got the shears with you," he replied, sharing a bit of rural New York farm wisdom.

We had both the shears and the saw with us, and it seemed like a good time to cut down a few ambitious Russian olives growing on a high ledge above us. It was a short but steep climb using eroded hand-holds. We found ourselves standing below ochre-, red-, and white-painted panels of antelope and Hopi figures. A round stone-and-mortar storage cyst in the narrow alcove once held dried corn and fruit throughout the winter; now it was empty and crowded by the trees.

Margarita and I walked to the end of the ledge. We talked about Margarita's marriage, which was headed for divorce. Her husband, whom I

Cornfield in the canyon.

had never met, was a Forest Service fire fighter who worked away from home most of the time. We talked about the young man with whom I was involved—a sweet relationship, but not one destined for longevity. We talked about our daughters growing up without fathers and about our philosophies of life. Finally, we took the saw and began to cut. In the crack at the back of the ledge grew a line of blue yucca and, in the damp moss of the sandstone seep, a tiny piñon. We cut the olives—ruthless water suckers—and took great joy in throwing them over the edge. We talked about reestablishing the irrigation system, and about bringing in Navajo and non-Navajo student groups to work.

"What do you think it would take for me to run the farm again, the way it used to be?" Margarita wondered. I thought briefly about my own land in New York and its idle acres before I answered. "A hell of a lot of courage, and a good deal of help."

Chapter 4

Sleeping Thunder

"Just look for the big pine tree," Chad Benally advised as he sketched a simple map on the back of a canyon leaflet. I picked up the map. It was a collection of seemingly incomprehensible squiggles and arrows, the kind I had grown accustomed to receiving whenever I asked for directions. Such a map would be clear only to someone with prior knowledge of the area, someone whose family lived around Canyon de Chelly for five generations, who remembered vanished landmarks and could recognize the unique characteristics of an individual tree.

It was October 1992. Charlie and I had just arrived back at Canyon de Chelly and had a hike through a canyon east of Chinle scheduled for the next day. We planned a short jaunt—just over the next mesa and around the bend—to see some Spanish-era inscriptions that Chad suspected were significant. As we stood at the desk in the visitor center, I looked at the map he'd just drawn for us. The "big pine tree" was near the "old hogan" after the "third side canyon" right beyond the "dry wash."

"Chad," I said, "why don't we meet at your house and all go to the trailhead in your truck?" He agreed. Chad and his family lived in an attractive enclave of government housing on the road between Chinle and Ganado, a development built on land donated by his in-laws. Half of the homes were "rent-to-buy," paid for over twenty-five years through a fifty-fifty partnership with the government. The rest were straight rentals.

Chad's house displayed the comfortable clutter of a family of six. TV, VCR, stereo, telephone, and numerous novels sat among Navajo rugs and kachinas. Chad's wife, Marilyn, worked as an administrator at the Chinle schools. She was also a seamstress who designed contemporary clothes along traditional lines. Part of the living room was devoted to her sewing and to the many awards she'd won at county and state exhibitions. Although Chad's in-laws maintained a summer sheep camp in the hills, this home had an air of permanence that was missing from the seasonal dwellings of Margarita's family.

It was a brilliant October morning when we started toward the trail-head. Chad wore a vivid blue Hawaiian-print shirt and blue shorts, set off by an elaborate red-and-black brace on his left knee. We bumped down a dirt track in his truck toward a distant canyon. The golden and mustard-colored leaves of the cottonwoods and the dry red leaves of the scrub oak fluttered audibly in the wind.

We parked the truck under an old piñon, pausing to search below it for some of the year's crop of nuts. It had been a bountiful year for piñons. On our way to the trail, we passed several grandmothers and children with buckets crawling under the trees to gather nuts. The crop was so abundant that the price was only half the usual three dollars per pound, and the nuts were big, moist, and flavorful.

The trail led down into a wash, through an Anasazi surface site littered with painted and coiled sherds, past rock art and historic inscriptions. We ambled up and down the sandy banks, and climbed to a ledge where Chad found a well-worn moccasin seven years earlier. It was still there, hidden under pack-rat rubble at the back of an overhang. Chad thought it might be early Navajo, from before the Long Walk. Several hours later, the sun sank low in the sky and I started thinking about heading back. I should have known better. It was always the case when hiking with Chad that, just as you began to tire, the real hiking began. Ahead was a small "fortress butte," the tallest out-cropping around, used by the Anasazi and the Navajos as a lookout and shelter. Two demolished hogan circles sat at the base, and in the distance we could see an old-style, forked-stick hogan. There was a prehistoric log ladder leading into a crack in the butte, then three rocks carved as steps. After that you had to hoist yourself up, using hands and buttocks to inch toward three logs wedged horizontally across the crack. With some effort Chad made it to the top, confirming that the long, high logs were still firmly placed in holes that had been axed out of the sandstone centuries before.

Large pieces of polychrome pottery dating back to the 1700s were evidence that this area had been farmed seasonally by the Hopis before the Navajos moved to the area from Diné Tah, their ancestral lands to the east. Once again, we stopped to look at a treasure left hidden by Chad years before—an almost complete bowl. We looked for an elusive rock art panel, just over the next mesa and up and down a couple of talus slopes. As Chad stood examining a mental map, Raven came circling low, calling. Another followed, as if checking the nature of the two-legged intruders standing on the high rocks in the late, blue afternoon.

We climbed along a rim to where the site should have been. Coyote had been there before us, tracks clearly visible in the damp earth. I paused to gather some ephedra, which I learned to use at home in place of commercial decongestants. "That's Mormon Tea," said Chad. "What do you call it in Navajo?" I asked. "Mormon Tea," he said, laughing.

We hiked some more and finally reached the edge of the canyon. Chad stood just beyond me, looking perplexed. The walls dropped 400 feet to the bottom, then rose again, just as high, 200 feet away on the other side. "Forgot about that other canyon," he said, deadpan.

We decided to turn back and postpone the "real" hike for another day. Chad's wife, Marilyn, asked Charlie to photograph the fourth annual "Breath of Autumn" benefit fashion show and spaghetti dinner that evening, and we had to be at the Chinle primary school by seven o'clock.

That evening, we entered the cafeteria building of the bright, airy school complex built to replace the dilapidated array of trailers and Quonset huts in use until the 1970s. Plunking down three dollars apiece for dinner, we joined the food service line and filled our plates.

The raised stage at the rear of the cafeteria was set off by a partition decorated with brightly colored butterflies, ice cream cones, and umbrellas. The sides were draped with long, tinsel-like curtains, and a patterned quilt was displayed at one side. Vases of paper flowers decorated the stage. As at so many events in the Southwest, the background music was a recording by flutist Carlos Nakai.

Charlie bustled about, photographing the kids backstage as they got ready for the fashion show and teaching Chad's older son how to use the camera. The kids who were already dressed peeked out from behind the partition. We waited for Sharon Watson, the current Miss Navajo Nation, to arrive and kick off the event. A high-school senior, Sharon was the third queen from Chinle to be chosen in as many years. "Navajo time," Chad said to me. At last, Sharon arrived in wine-red velveteen, turquoise jewelry, and a turquoise-and-silver crown. Marilyn introduced her, first in English, then in Navajo. Miss Navajo Nation, also speaking in two languages, introduced herself in the traditional manner, giving her name, family, and clans.

The models, in clothes donated by the Gallup K-Mart, were shy. Most of them didn't linger on stage but walked quickly across, cut a fast turn, and then ducked into the back before Charlie could take a full-face picture. Even more reluctant were the entertainers who sang and danced between the acts. Nevertheless, they were greeted with enthusiastic applause, especially Greta Joe, the Chinle High School Princess, who reigned locally while Miss Navajo Nation toured the reservation. It was an honor for a young woman to be chosen Princess. But it was also a drain on the resources of her family, who had to accompany her to innumerable powwows and other events during the course of the year, repaying kindnesses through giveaways.

Greta Joe, Chinle High School Princess

Greta Joe's father worked for the Navajo Nation Highway Department. He explained his frustrations:

> They keep setting aside more money for roads, but it seems like we never get a project finished. They're always making five-year plans, and then somebody new takes over and the plans get lost. Even when one gets approved, first we have to wait for archaeological and environmental clearances. The only people working this year are the archaeologists. Half the budget's been spent, but we haven't gotten around to building any roads.

When I asked Greta's father about his hopes for her future, he said,

> I'd like to see her continue in school; that's important. But in a guarded atmosphere. Maybe a school in Utah I heard about. I'm not sure about what they learn off the reservation. I'd like Greta to go to a school where she would be free from outside influences, from values that are not the ones of her own culture. My generation, you know, we still remember the boarding schools.

Boarding school tales loom large in the childhood reminiscences of many middle-aged Navajos. Although the 1930s saw the establishment of reservation day schools to replace the substandard boarding schools that preceded them, insufficient funding in the years after World War II forced the locally run community schools out of existence. In the 1950s, twenty years after the idea of cross-cultural education was adopted as federal policy, the drive to assimilate Native American children was renewed.

Chad, Margarita, and others who attended elementary school in the 1950s vividly remember the arrival of strangers whose job it was to take them away from their families, to be housed and educated at boarding schools near Fort Defiance or Shiprock. The children's long hair was cut off at school, and they were forbidden to speak their native language or wear traditional clothing. Almost all speak of attempts to escape those dreaded prisons.

Chad's story was typical. "They came for us in a wagon," he said. "I wondered why my mom made me go, but I guess she didn't have much choice. She didn't speak English. They took me to that boarding school, and after a little while I left. I walked and I walked for what seemed like days. I was on foot and had no food." He paused. "Maybe it wasn't so far; I was little then. Finally I reached my hogan. They were waiting for me there, the biligáana. They took me right back to that school."

Margarita's story was similar. She remembered the wagon, and the haircuts, and how much she loved coming back home to herd sheep in the summer.

The Treaty of 1868 created a "special relationship" between the Navajo Nation and the US government. In exchange for a promise to "remain at peace" with the United States, a reservation was established for the Navajos, and a number of entitlement programs were instituted. The first of these was a commitment to provide one teacher for every thirty children of school age so that Navajo youth might receive an "English education."

In 1924, the US government granted citizenship to all Native Americans. The rights and responsibilities guaranteed by the Fourteenth Amendment were extended to the Navajo people, including the obligation to serve in the armed forces. Both Arizona and New Mexico, however, withheld the Navajos' right to vote. Arizona maintained that Navajos living on reservation trust lands were wards of the government and, therefore, could not be considered Arizona residents. New Mexico denied Navajos the vote because they paid no taxes. Court cases finally granted all reservation Navajos the right to vote in 1948, but for decades afterward literacy tests continued to prevent many of the People from voting.

Today, Navajos have access to all federal benefits and services available to any other American citizen, including social programs such as food stamps, nutritional programs, and other public assistance transfer payments. In addition, they are entitled to educational and other benefits resulting from treaty agreements. This dual entitlement covers health care, provided at Indian Health Service facilities, and housing and other assistance from programs funded by the Bureau of Indian Affairs.

In 1975, the federal government passed Public Law No. 93/638, the Indian Self-Determination and Education Assistance Act, designed to give tribes greater power in the design and implementation of educational and social programs. The goal was to eliminate "federal domination of the Indian service programs which has served to retard rather than enhance the progress of the Indian people." Although more than half of all BIA programs today are administered by the tribes themselves, many tribes fear that Congress will use this act to withdraw its support of Indian sovereignty and eliminate its special relationship with Native American peoples.

For most Navajos, boarding school was a loathsome experience, and there was a growing demand for community public day schools after World War II. A major barrier was that Native Americans did not pay land-based school taxes. Non-natives who used reservation land were taxed, but the funds provided only a spotty base since some districts received high revenues while others did not. Thus, the establishment of public education required a formula for support from both the federal government and the individual states. New school systems flourished during the 1960s, thanks to "Great Society" programs. By the late 1970s, however, cutbacks left many school districts floundering in the wake of increased enrollments and decreased funding.

During the last thirty years, Navajo education policy has emphasized development of a curriculum that would preserve traditional culture and language while also preparing young people for the labor market most of them will enter. As in the past, certain practical barriers hamper the establishment of quality education on the reservation. Schools are still heavily staffed by Anglo teachers hired by the BIA. The tribe has been slow to produce its own professionals, in part because young people must leave the reservation to attend four-year colleges and are frequently ill prepared for the experiences they encounter there. Diné College is considering establishing a four-year program at Tsaile that would allow students to remain near home, close to family and familiar demands, as they prepare to become teachers.

"I don't want to go, Mom. I don't want to spend the weekend in that boring place," said Margarita's daughter, Carla. She had arrived home from Tsaile Junior High on Friday afternoon to find out her mother planned to spend the weekend at the Park Service housing enclave.

Fluent in Navajo and English, Carla was equally adept in a teenage language that seemed to cross cultural lines. She loved to dance and played the same music as my daughter did. Carla could move fluidly between a Navajo Song and Dance and a disco style. In the autumn, her week was structured around basketball games and practice. This was her first year as a member of the Tsaile School's women's team. She was tall and getting taller, her face becoming softly beautiful as she grew into womanhood. The following year Carla would ride the bus more than fifty miles each day in order to attend high school in Chinle. She wasn't thrilled by the idea, and Margarita was considering sending her to a boarding school in Tuba City instead. "How can you do that?" I asked Margarita, remembering her own stories about boarding school.

Margarita assured me that conditions had changed. "They don't chain you to the bed any more or cut your hair," she said. "And I just don't know if I want her at Chinle." I understood her anxieties about finding the right school. Noreen's older boys were not doing well at Chinle High. It was big and impersonal, unlike the smaller junior high at Tsaile.

Charlie and I arrived at Margarita's "urban" home in the government housing complex, close to the Lukachukai-Tsaile intersection, just moments before Carla. The neat, well-kept, two-bedroom house was filled with people, including Margarita and Carla; Margarita's sister, Alicia; and her young son, Everett; two other friends; and Charlie and me. As so often happened when we visited Navajo homes, it felt like a gathering but not a crowd.

We all spent the night and woke to the sounds of Navajo language and country music on KTNN radio. Margarita made tortillas in the kitchen while the kids watched a Daffy Duck video in the living room.

There was no TV reception without cable, and the nearest movie theater was in Gallup, but videos could be rented at most trading posts and convenience stores on the reservation.

When breakfast was ready, I knocked on Carla's bedroom door, behind which pounded the repetitive rhythm of a rap tune. Carla opened the door and I glimpsed the shiny black bedroom set her father had given her for her thirteenth birthday. It celebrated her maturity, much as the Kinaaldá ceremony had done two years before. Carla was dressed in tennis shoes and a sweat suit, ready to walk down to a battered basketball hoop at the end of the road.

"I hope my mom doesn't remember that she wanted to go back to Chinle for the weekend," she said in an undertone to Charlie and me. Charlie turned to her. "We're already talking about stopping at your Grandma Karen's to visit, so I'm confident that it'll be a day or two before we get back to Park Service headquarters," he said conspiratorially. Carla laughed and headed out the door in search of friends or relatives who might be interested in shooting a few hoops.

One of the advantages of a large family is always having enough people around for competitive sports. Visitors hiking in the canyon were often puzzled when they saw two tall juniper posts in the middle of the wash. Were they some kind of high-water markers or channel guides to direct drivers through the sand? But anyone who happened to look down from the rim on a Sunday afternoon would probably see a net attached to the posts and a family setting out a picnic to one side as a volleyball game began.

The routine was a little different on Saturdays, at least until the onset of cold weather. Softball tournaments began early and continued throughout the day, especially at the field outside of Chinle. By 10 AM the field was surrounded by pickup trucks, blue tarp sunshades stretched before them in preparation for an all-day event. In fact, it was often hard to find a canyon guide on softball Saturdays when women and men of all ages competed. One family, anxious to have as much practice and playing time as possible, convinced their grandma to reduce the size of her cornfields and put in a full-scale baseball diamond.

Softball and volleyball dominated the summer months; basketball and football took over in the fall. Noreen's oldest son, Eddie, played football for Chinle High School. Though the family stayed on the peninsula, preparing to move the sheep to winter camp, on Friday game nights everyone piled into the pickup to watch him play. They looked forward to the following Friday, when they would cheer on the Chinle team during the annual homecoming game.

Boxing was also popular among the young people. Bill Yazzie, one of the Park Service's Navajo law enforcement rangers, coached both girls and boys for state and national competitions. Bill believed that boxing built confidence and character in youngsters who were struggling to form their identities in a time when old ways were fast disappearing and new ways had not yet been defined.

Earlier that week, I visited a boxing practice session in a tiny yard in the Park Service enclave. The ring was made of four pieces of pipe, upended and connected by ropes covered in black electrical tape. Boys and girls from four to fifteen years old took turns in the ring, guided by Bill and another young Navajo. Wearing helmets and mouth protectors, the youngsters sparred with the coaches or worked out with a heavy punching bag. The boxing team was good and hoped to take the state title.

When they weren't at practice, the team was busy preparing a float for a parade to publicize Child Abuse Prevention Week on the reservation. On the day of the parade, I arrived early, but it was half past ten before the first floats started down the road from Baldwin's Mini-mart to the old elementary school complex.

The route was lined with preschoolers representing Head Start units from throughout the Chinle chapter, attended by the many mothers and grandmothers who kept the program going. When the floats rolled by, the

Navajo parents with newborn.

Chinle and Tsaile School Princesses threw candy to the crowd, and kids looked questioningly at their chaperones before running to grab it. The Head Start programs were burgeoning to accommodate the growing number of Navajo children. Despite the economic burdens of childrearing, babies were still cherished, and extended families still provided an effective source of love and care.

As I looked at the preschoolers lined in front of their Head Start bus, I recalled an incident that had occurred during my first summer as a Canyon de Chelly park ranger. Gloria, who worked in the office at the visitor center, approached and said, "I have three kids, Jeanne, and I'm pregnant again. I don't know if I want this one. We're pretty comfortable the way we are. How do you get an abortion?" I didn't know Gloria very well and was surprised by her disclosure and her question. "I don't know how it works on the reservation, but I can find out if you'd like," I said.

During the week, I learned it was not possible to have an abortion on the reservation; you had to go to Albuquerque or Flagstaff, and the Indian Health Service wouldn't pay for it. Gloria thanked me for the information and said she would think about it.

Two weeks later, I wandered into the office near closing. Gloria was getting ready to leave, pick up her children, and go to a rodeo. She was an active mother, participating with all her family in Navajo social dances, concerned that they maintain their culture and their language.

"How's it going?" I asked. "Well," said Gloria, sitting back down for a minute. "I've thought about it and thought about it. And as much as I was settled with the way our family was, not to have this baby is against everything I believe in. We've got enough love in our family to see another one through." Gloria had a boy.

The parade made its way through Chinle. Bill Yazzie and the boxing float brought up the rear, followed by a Navajo Tribal Police vehicle. Like several other rangers, Bill began working for Park Service law enforcement after a stint in the Tribal Police. Visitors to the reservation were often perplexed by the plethora of law enforcement agencies. A frequent question was, "Who's in charge here?" This was especially the case at Canyon de Chelly, where the situation was more complex than on the rest of the reservation. The Park Service's primary concerns were to ensure safety and maintain the integrity of the ruins. Crimes against property, domestic violence, and substance abuse anywhere on the reservation fell within the purview of the Navajo Tribal Police. However, if the infraction involved a sentence of more than six months, the case had to be heard in a federal court. The FBI investigated capital crimes. In such instances, ideally, there was cooperation between tribal and federal law enforcement. While state police units were occasionally seen on the reservation, they had no clear-cut jurisdiction there.

Jurisdictional debates were related, in part, to the tribe's ambiguous legal status. The Navajo Nation was governed by an elected president and a tribal council, but this tribal government did not enjoy the same rights and privileges as state and county units and could be excluded from certain benefits and programs. Moreover, in spite of the policy of self-determination, any significant proposal adopted by the council had to be approved by the BIA. Certain other areas, such as religious freedom, also fell into a jurisdictional morass, and it was unclear in some instances whether state, federal, or tribal law should prevail.

When I returned to the reservation in October 1993, I was introduced to the newest members of Margarita's family: three tiny babies, each placidly bundled in a polished cedar cradleboard. "It's the Navajo car seat," somebody joked. "Only we had it long before the biligáana did." For each baby there was a beaming grandma. One of them was Karen, Margarita's mother, who stood behind her daughter Lora's newborn son, Isaiah.

I made a cultural blunder during the summer by buying tiny yellow sleeping gowns, realizing just before presenting the gifts to Lora that usually nothing was made or bought for a baby before its birth. The same custom applied to the cradleboard, which was often made by one of the men of the family only after the baby was safely in this world.

Lora planned to have her baby in the traditional way, in the family hogan at Black Rock. She contacted a medicine man about the birthing ceremony, and Karen and the other older women brought their knowledge of numerous births to the experience. At the same time, Lora was also attending the prenatal clinic at the Indian Health Service Hospital in Fort Defiance.

The obstetrics department is undoubtedly the most progressive area in the Indian Health Service reservation hospitals. I met two non-Navajo nurse-midwives who worked at the Chinle facility and learned they were dedicated to blending Western medical practice with traditional Navajo healing. Patients were encouraged to use Western medicines and methods in conjunction with Navajo ceremonies and herbs. The nurse-midwives who provided primary care were very committed to their work. They realized they were acquiring a valuable body of knowledge in women's medicine from their patients as they became familiar with the traditional natural remedies and practices surrounding pregnancy and childbirth.

"These women seem to have a matter-of-fact relationship with birthing," said a young midwife from Wisconsin who worked at Chinle. "Last week a woman came to the hospital in the early stages of labor. I examined her and told her I thought she had a few hours until the birth. She checked her watch and told me she'd be back around midnight. There was a Song and Dance at the high school, and she didn't want to miss it."

But Lora's labor, her first, had not gone smoothly. She was at Black Rock, all prepared for a home birth. The day dawned warm and lazy, and so did Lora's labor. Fifteen hours later she still had not progressed. The medicine man arrived. By the next morning, Lora was in great discomfort, having regular contractions, but the labor just dragged on. Finally the medicine man spoke: "You are a modern woman. You have lived away from here for many years, learned many new ways. I've listened to you, and what I hear is that you are not meant to give birth here, in the old way. If you go to the hospital, this baby will come."

Sad and exhausted, Lora was driven off the peninsula to the birthing room in Fort Defiance. Isaiah was born soon afterward, healthy and heavy, and it was truly a modern birth. Lora's Aunt Ellen—Noreen's mother—tied the cord. Thirty-five-millimeter photos and a videotape captured the event and the joy of the family as they welcomed a new life into the world.

The Navajos are the fastest-growing Native American nation in the United States, with birth rates twice those of the rest of the country. Though economic conditions on the reservation might prompt a desire to limit family size, tradition and intense nationalism are powerful constraints on this tendency.

The past decades have brought continuing modernization to the reservation, including better roads and communication systems, potable water, electrification, and access to media, technology, and education. Anti-poverty programs in the 1960s and early 1970s increased literacy. Improved health facilities extended Western medical care into the area and reduced infant mortality. In spite of these changes, wage-labor opportunities on the reservation did not expand, and families continue to depend on a combination of service-related jobs, subsistence activities, and off-reservation labor. Kin groups remain heavily reliant on contributions from income-generating members.

Although Navajo women have moved into the job market only recently, they have always had a great deal of control over their own lives. One woman told me, "When it comes to running the household, our lives are little different from the way they were when the men were always off as hunters and warriors. Now they hunt in a different fashion, in construction jobs in Phoenix, but they are still gone."

The increased migration of young people seeking jobs and higher education off the reservation has resulted in a rejection of both tradition and traditional values. Navajo women have become heavily involved in wage labor, especially in the service industry, and show a high commitment to education, factors often associated with fertility decline. Average family size dropped from the five to ten children of their mothers' era to three to five.

Greater accessibility of birth control and abortion on the reservation during the 1970s contributed to this decline. In 1955, the US Public Health Service assumed responsibility for services to Indian communities, an extension of the nineteenth-century trust responsibility. With easier availability, use of fertility control measures was high during the 1970s, especially among certain age groups. Although abortion is in conflict with traditional Navajo values, it was utilized until the passage of the Hyde Amendment in 1977, which made such federally funded surgical procedures illegal. A bureaucratic loophole allowed extension of services through 1981, but since then it has not been possible to obtain an abortion on the reservation, and Indian Health Service funds cannot be used for off-reservation operations. Since most Navajos have no other health benefits, and since the nearest cities with services are at distant edges of the reservation, pregnancy interruption is no longer a viable option.

Children are the most valued asset of the Navajo people. Although family planning is still easily obtained, traditional teachings place serious constraints on the use of methods to control births, particularly abortion. Today, many Navajos returning to the reservation from school, as well as those raised off the reservation, show a resurgence of interest in traditional beliefs that assert that an unborn child is alive. To have an abortion is to kill that new person. As a result, evil will return and harm the

Children . . . the promise of the Navajo Nation.

mother at some later time. Young people embracing old ways are reluctant to interfere with fertility.

"There's my mom!" yelled Margarita suddenly, as we drove past the turnoff to Park Service headquarters. "Pull over, can you?"

We were driving back to Tsaile with a car full of groceries when we saw Karen coming toward us in the pickup, her husband Leonard at the wheel. Margarita and I spent an hour at Basha's buying food for the one hundred people due to attend a Native American Church meeting later that evening. Because she was tired of mutton, Margarita had asked me to cook for the group: twenty pounds of old-fashioned biligáana meatloaf.

Margarita ran across the road to talk to her mother while I waited in the idling car. Finally, Margarita darted back across the lane of traffic. "She's going to Basha's to get some mutton," she reported. "She heard you were making meatloaf and says it just won't do. I told her we bought some mutton, but she's certain it won't be enough. She wants everything to be the way it should."

"For your parents, you never grow up," I said. "They're certain you can never do things right without their help." Margarita nodded in agreement.

A year ago, when Margarita's life had seemed uncertain and unsettled, her mother arranged a Native American Church Peyote Ceremony for her. Now, twelve months later, Margarita's path seemed more certain, and it was time to thank the Holy People for a full and harmonious year.

It was just after dawn when Charlie and I left Margarita's house in Tsaile, our rented Geo Metro loaded with shovels, butane, rakes, water, and cleaning equipment. Almost immediately, we were hailed by two of Margarita's teenaged nephews looking for a ride to Black Rock. They piled into the back seat and we drove the short distance to the solar housing, where we picked up Margarita's sister, Lora, and her baby, Isaiah, happily bundled into his cradleboard. They, too, got into the back seat. Six-year-old Everett, the son of Margarita's other sister, Alicia, climbed into my lap in front.

The older boys were excited about the upcoming ceremony. They quietly practiced a selection of ceremonial songs as we bumped our way along the packed mud leading to Black Rock. Everett talked nonstop on my lap, providing a running commentary on the social history of every mile of the road. We passed a spot where Charlie and I had picked up all three boys while they were herding sheep the previous summer, soaking wet and chilled after a sudden downpour. We had given them popcorn and a dry towel and sent them off to find the flock. Now we all laughed, remembering.

Water still remained in a small pond outside the turn-off to Karen's Black Rock summer house. The livestock looked healthy, well-fed beef cattle sheltering their young as they grazed close to the road. We passed by the windmill and tank where Margarita washed clothes as a child. It was surrounded by wiry sage and drying rabbitbrush, forming a frame for graffiti on the tank that proclaimed "heavy metal."

The enclave contained three hogans, two cabins, and a large shade house. There were solar collectors on the roof of one of the cabins, but these had not worked in more than three years. Lora remembered a brief period with solar-generated electricity before the batteries failed and could not be replaced. Several cracked windows in the house were mended with duct tape.

Margarita arrived in her little Suzuki Samurai. She and I rolled two barrels of clean water out of the back of the vehicle, then got to work removing everything from the one-room cabin. Charlie and the boys grabbed hammers and an ax and began to dismantle the shade house, which leaned precariously to the east, in preparation for a hasty rebuilding.

A blue pickup arrived with the lodge poles for the tipi that would shelter the NAC meeting. The all-night ceremony was a time to talk about what has passed and what is to come, and to ask for continued blessings in the company of friends and relatives. Drums and singing would provide the background for this meditation on one's relationship to all living things. Peyote helped to bring the participants closer to the Holy People in a setting that combined Native American imagery with that of Christianity. I had been surprised to learn that many of my acquaintances, including young people and elders, professionals and teachers, canyon guides and Catholics, were NAC members.

Some of the family was busy clearing the space where the tipi would be raised, on the site of an old corral. They spread the ever-present goat dung to make a flat surface and watered down the sandy earth to keep the dust under control. Charlie was joined by more of the men from Margarita's family. With the help of a roll of baling wire and some strong backs, they quickly rebuilt the shade house.

The women continued cleaning the house, bringing box after box of children's toys out to the edge of the sage for examination. Alicia sorted through the mementos of her children's early years, when they lived in the house with their grandma. Though she threw most of the toys into a large black trash bag, she saved one or two items with special meaning.

"Look at this! This was Dezbah's favorite stuffed bear," she said, referring to her now-teenaged daughter. She reached into another box and pulled out an old clown mask. On impulse, a third sister put on the mask, ran over to where her mother, Karen, was gathering firewood, and gave the older woman a hug.

Close to dinner time, four men—NAC members—arrived to raise the tipi. As they started to work, Karen unearthed a twenty-five-pound sack of Bluebird flour and quickly mixed bread dough. Then, using the dis-

carded cross beams of the shade house, she started a fire on the mesa in front of the cabin. With the help of her granddaughters, Carla and Dezbah, she began to make a huge quantity of bread. A side of mutton also materialized, and the ribs were placed on the fire to cook. Looking out from inside the cabin, where I stood washing an endless mound of dishes, pots, and pans, I saw the tipi was already up, dwarfing the round, squat hogan.

I finished the dishes and walked over to peek in through the tipi opening, feeling shy and reverent, like a tourist entering a foreign church. Inside, one of the men had already sketched out the crescent shape of the altar. He invited me in, and I sat quietly, imagining the sound of drums and the smell of juniper fire that would fill the space the following night.

Earlier that day, Margarita asked if I wanted to come into the tipi the next day. It was a tempting invitation, but I turned it down. To attend meant to participate in the entire ceremony, and I didn't know if I had the ability to sit quietly and listen to the Navajo language and drumming for twelve hours. "Remember me and my family during the ceremony," I told Margarita.

Native American religious ceremonies and practices are as diverse as Native American peoples themselves. Over the years, the US government and other representatives of Anglo culture have attempted to substitute Christian beliefs for Native American practices, often through the use of force. These efforts intensified in the 1890s with the rise of the Ghost Dance religion, a revitalization movement that looked to a return to the days before white domination. The Ghost Dance movement was pan-tribal and threatened to unify Native American groups. Attempts to eliminate it resulted in the massacre of three hundred Lakota by US troops at Wounded Knee, South Dakota, in 1890.

By 1892, the BIA authored the Indian Religious Crimes Regulation, which made it a crime to participate in any type of Native American dancing or ceremony. Violators faced ten days in jail or ten days without rations. The rule remained in effect until 1921. After that, more than five decades were to pass before Congress recognized that the term "religion" extended to wide areas of Indian culture and practice.

The Indian Religious Freedom Act of 1978, designed to "protect and preserve for Native Americans their inherent right of freedom to believe, express, and exercise the traditional religions," provided a minimal level of religious freedom. Specifically, it authorized reevaluation of any federal policies that might curtail access to sacred sites on federal land or prevent traditional ceremonies and the possession of sacred objects.

Opposite page: Making fry bread to feed those coming to the ceremony.

Unfortunately, the act has no enforcement section, so while practices may be reviewed, it is unlikely that action will be taken. Moreover, the protection is federal and has no effect at the state level. States may continue to deny tribes access to sacred land, prevent use of sacred objects such as eagle feathers, prohibit prison inmates from holding ceremonies, and refuse to excuse children from school to attend ceremonies. To date, the only portion of the Indian Religious Freedom Act that has been clarified concerns the sacramental use of peyote in the Native American Church. As a result of a 1994 amendment to the act, states cannot prohibit the use of peyote in appropriate ceremonies.

"I don't know what we're gonna do with the sheep," said Margarita matter-of-factly. Margarita, Charlie, and I stood near a small juniper fire, warming ourselves against the midnight chill. It was only mid October, but the nighttime temperatures were in the twenties, and frost kissed the piñon and ponderosa of the high country. Thunder was fast asleep. Four days passed since I delivered five heavy trays of meatloaf to the NAC meeting. It was the weekend again, and we were in attendance for a *Ye'ii'bechai* healing ceremony.

I looked at Margarita curiously. "What sheep?" She leaned closer to the fire, warming her hands as she spoke. "I just talked to Noreen. They asked her to be lead dancer for her group. That means that she's got to dance at least three times, probably staying until four-thirty in the morning. It also means that the patient's family is gonna give her a sheep."

I nodded, thinking about the luggage space in the Geo Metro. It was just about the right size. "Is it dead or alive?" I asked calmly. "It's a live one," Margarita told me, surprised that I needed to ask. "It's a big one." She looked at me, and we laughed and decided to worry about it later.

A series of small fires edged a grassy runway leading to a large hogan. I could hear faint sounds of singing from within as we waited for the first dancers to appear. I marveled at Margarita's ability to stay awake through these all-night gatherings, go back to work for a few days, and then stay up all night again.

We arrived at about eleven-thirty and parked the Metro amidst a sea of pickups. Looking around the groups of people huddled near the many fires, I saw there were only two other biligáana. As on other occasions, I felt uncomfortable, as though I had come to be a spectator at someone's private consultation with his doctor. Even after three years, I wasn't sure if Charlie and I were welcome.

The fires burned brightly, but there was no central bonfire as there had been at the summertime Squaw Dance. At the far end of the corridor stood a circular brush arbor, the Yei house. In the glow of the firelight from within I could just discern figures moving about, but their features and their identities were hidden to us.

This was the last night of a nine-day healing ceremony, the night that the Yeis and Talking God danced. As we waited, speaking in quiet tones, four dancers approached the hogan. They were all male, dressed in white clay and elaborate kilts, masked and feathered, and wearing broad collars of fresh spruce. Each carried a gourd rattle in one hand, a spruce bough in the other. Deerskin medicine pouches hung across their shoulders, and foxtails dangled almost to their feet, which were encased in high moccasins. They stood, silent and motionless. Haashch'éélti'i—Talking God— was with them, clad in buckskins and, like the other men, masked.

Moon was a lazy half, lying on her side. Her long beams mixed with firelight as the dancers were joined by the medicine man and the patient, a young boy, who sat swaddled in a blanket. The healer was tall, gray-haired, and robed. Slowly the Ye'ii'bechai began to dance, singing, shaking rattles, repeating purposeful steps four times before returning to the Yei house.

The patient entered the hogan, and the guests began to talk and move about. Across from us, a small trailer that served as a concession stand sold coffee and snacks for the long night's vigil. A loudspeaker system gave a running commentary in Navajo on what was taking place. Suddenly the voice switched to English.

"I realize there are some Anglos present," said the booming voice. My heart dropped. How embarrassing it would be to be asked to leave; to be told we were unwelcome. "Please don't take any pictures," the voice continued.

Charlie and I looked at each other. They were talking about us! We nodded in the darkness, agreeing that we wouldn't have considered doing so during a ceremony. The voice continued. "I want to thank you for taking the time out of your busy schedules to come and support my grandson for this time of healing. Thank you for coming. You are welcome."

I looked up in amazement. It was as if the speaker had sensed my awkwardness and gone out of his way to dispel it. I realized then that healing was a community endeavor, one in which all one's friends joined to give support. When one is ill, or out of harmony, he or she is not left to suffer alone. I had come to Arizona this time after canceling a surgical procedure about which I had doubts. Here, in the firelight and darkness, the mystery of the night was multiplied and the healing reached from the patient to encircle all those waiting, myself included.

Thirty minutes later, the sound of the gourd rattles began again. This round there were more than twenty dancers, paired men and women. The men were dressed like the first group, the women in skirts and full blouses. We spotted a masked dancer in mossy green, with the body and movements of Aunt Noreen. She danced with her partner at the head of a long line as the patient again waited in his seat near the door of the hogan. The dance was slow, solemn, and methodical, comprised of paired Ye'ii'bechai who were blessed by the patient between repetitions.

As we watched in fascination, we noticed a solitary dancer in a costume that was the reverse of all the others. His foxtail waved from his mouth instead of his bottom. The dancer pranced from spectator to spectator, performing elaborate pantomimes that left the crowd laughing. When he danced, he was one step behind. When he sang, he was one beat behind.

"What's he all about?" Charlie wondered aloud. "It's the clown, the trickster," I explained. "He mocks the entire ceremony and lets you know that the sacred ways are not inflexible." In his bawdy dance, the clown reminded us that what was up was also down, what was here was also there, what was life-threatening could become life-giving.

At dawn, the sheep went home to Black Rock with us to become mutton for the new day's dinner. Noreen had danced all night, a masked figure moving through the moonlit hours. Watching her and the other Yeis, I sent my prayers to the young patient and shared the night's blessings in return. I saw no human dancers that night—not Noreen, nor the Trickster, nor Talking God. The players in that frosty clearing were the Yeis, alive and earthbound, endowed with the immeasurable power of timeless ceremony.

Although the October days were still long and golden in the cottonwood sunshine, winter approached. The sheep would soon be at their winter camps, the fall piñon nuts dried and stored near the apricots of summer.

"You know, there was a biligáana who came out here last summer and wanted a ceremony," Margarita told me as she swept aside the layers of russet dust settled on her battered kitchen table. We were down at the junction enjoying a final visit before I had to return east to finish the fall semester.

"I went to this medicine man and asked him if he'd do it, and he said yes. But he told me it would cost the man $300 for one night's sing. I asked why the fee was higher than for a Navajo. You know what he answered?" I shook my head; I was surprised that he would consider doing the ceremony in the first place. "He said that when he does a sing for one of us, he knows that we have at one time been in balance, that something has interfered with our knowledge of this land and our relationship with the Holy People. There is *hózhó*, it has been disturbed, it must be reestablished. For white people, though, it is different. You are so far away from harmony that he must first work to bring you to a base, to a starting point. You were not raised with our traditions and our beliefs, and so, to help you in our fashion, he must first clear away the residue of your own way of life, the chaos, the uncertainty, the disturbance. Then, and only then, can he begin to heal you." The explanation seemed logical, the price not unreasonable. Three hundred dollars for an all-night sing was a bargain, a down payment on understanding in a rapidly changing world.

Margarita opened a cabinet and took out a can of dried Navajo tea. "How's your family?" she asked. "Are you going to bring Rachel out for her Kinaaldá?" I shook my head. "No chance. She won't leave that horse," I answered. Completely devoted to her horse, my daughter had not traveled with me since our summer together at Canyon de Chelly.

"And your man?" Margarita continued. "Not perfect," I said sadly. "And your mother?" I shrugged. "Things are getting worse. She's off in her own world a lot of the time."

"You need to bring her out here for a ceremony—a blackening."

I told Margarita about my mother's journeys into a place that was inaccessible to the rest of us. Margarita explained that the blackening ceremony was designed for that type of situation, in which ghosts were everywhere. I even talked to my mother about it during one of her coherent periods, but the illness had progressed too fast, and now she could no longer travel. "I sent her some ghost beads," I said, referring to the dried juniper berry necklaces sold on the reservation. Placed under a pillow, they are believed to prevent nightmares and keep ghosts from invading one's sleep. "I really wanted her to come out here and meet your mom. They have the same kind of spirit."

After a light dinner, Margarita and I walked partway up the Yei Trail. In the low light of evening, the canyon walls were a thick dusky rose, dotted with muted blue-green. The sun sank slowly through a ragged bank of clouds, and its rays turned the layers of mesa into three-dimensional steps. There was a steady hum of vehicles from the road on the south rim, as persistent as the dusk wind across the rock. In the distance, a few lights began to glow in Chinle.

We turned and retraced our footsteps in the gathering darkness, picking our way carefully down the deep steps, those ancient ledges filled with sand and lengthening shadow. Back on level ground, we walked in silence to Margarita's waiting Suzuki Samurai. Then, locking in the hubs and gunning the engine, we plowed through the chill and mounded mud of the wash and out of the canyon. Our separate lives mingling, we drove into the oncoming winter.

Epilogue

Reflecting Pools

Winter 1996–1997

In the summer of 1991, twenty of my students from the State University of New York traveled to Canyon de Chelly with me to join members of Margarita's family and clan at her place near the junction. Though the students looked forward to the opportunity to learn about Navajo culture from the Navajo people, they soon realized that they were to play a reciprocal role for Margarita's young nieces and nephews. Sharing work, meals, music, games, and dance, the two groups spent three days in an exchange of ideas and customs. Residents from throughout the canyon and surrounding areas dropped by when they heard about the visiting biligáana, turning us into the objects of curiosity that the endless stream of tour trucks habitually made of the canyon residents.

It was a wonderful, sometimes difficult experience. Grandmothers marveled at the sight of men cooking, watching them add innumerable spices and vegetables to a typically bland mutton stew. Many of the students were vegetarians who, as good anthropologists, broke with their own traditions to eat meat. Several tried their hand at shaping bread, spinning the dough in the air with impressive East Coast pizza-making finesse.

"We don't play with our food!" scolded Margarita's mother, Karen. She went on to correct one of the other cooks, who was stirring a pot of stew. "You don't stir with a knife. You cut with a knife," she told him, as Margarita translated.

There were times when we visitors fumbled, inadvertently hurting or offending those who had opened their lives to us. For instance, when we climbed a particularly difficult trail, stumbling and searching for the right line up the talus, a student commented that he didn't think a human being had been up that trail in years. "We use this trail every day," said Margarita, startled by his thoughtlessness.

But there were other moments, moments of understanding and shared peace. One student later wrote: "This morning we listened to Grandma Karen pray for all of us. I realized that . . . we are all brothers and sisters. Faces are different, but people are not. We are all one. There is no real difference. I did not need a translation."

Among our group that summer was a Japanese exchange student, an exuberant young man who hailed the People as long-lost cousins. While the Navajos were not ready to embrace him as a relative, they spent hours talking with him about what it was like to be a stranger, an outsider in another culture.

"Say something in Japanese! Sing a song," Noreen urged.

The young man complied happily, delighting his audience with a moving Japanese rendition of "Rudolf, the Red-Nosed Reindeer."

The following spring, one of Margarita's nephews was chosen to visit Japan as a representative of the Navajo Nation. It was a huge proposition: to leave the reservation, to venture beyond Phoenix, to cross an ocean, to visit a completely alien land. The family met and talked long and hard, considering the possibility from every perspective, as one examines a faceted stone. In the end, they drew on the experience of the summer before, their meeting with the American students and with one from Japan in particular. They agreed to let him go.

When he returned, the youngster described his journey. "Auntie," he told Margarita, wide-eyed, "everywhere I went I was so famous!" He thought Japan a crowded and busy place, one he would not like to live in.

Margarita and family during the student program.

When I pressed him for details, though, he was reluctant to speak, to stress his experience over that of his siblings and cousins. But his trip to Japan was just one of the journeys that the young people of Margarita's family would make that year.

In August of 1992, Carla Dawson and her cousin, Dezbah, arrived for a two-week visit to my home in upstate New York. I met their plane at the airport in Syracuse and, as we drove across the miles of rolling, verdant hills, the girls were astonished. What were all these tiny towns with ramshackle white buildings leaning lazily toward evening? "Jeanne," Carla asked in her soft, teasing voice, "Where's New York?"

We picked up my daughter, Rachel, at the horse farm where she had a summer job and stopped for two cheese-and-pepperoni pizzas on the way home. The pizzas spilled over the sides of their cardboard boxes, filling the car with an East Coast aroma. A new sign in front of our house dubbed it the "Evening Inn Farm," and in the mother-of-pearl dusk it bid the travelers welcome.

It rained that first night, and Carla coaxed the other girls into a midnight roll in the thick, green grass. I was awakened by the sound of their laughter mixed with the steady patter of raindrops, the gentle downpour on soft lawn that would be a desert luxury. During the next days, joined by a teenaged friend of Rachel's, the girls wandered the streets together, going to malls and movies, or dancing in the living room when the adults weren't looking.

Early one morning, we piled into the car and drove "downstate" to catch a bus to New York City. On the way we stopped for a brief visit at a sprawling suburban home with a swimming pool and a twenty-five-year mortgage, all supported by a two-income family. The girls, including Rachel, were impressed. But as our bus bumped along the New Jersey Turnpike, we counted the hours of commuting it would take to support that kind of life, and some of the glamour vanished.

As we approached the city, the bus entered the tiled, looming gullet of the Lincoln Tunnel. "We're driving under the river?" Dezbah asked, fascinated "How?" Although I had lived in New York for more than twenty-five years, I was still confounded by roads that went under rivers. The explanation I offered was decidedly vague.

Moments later, we arrived at the Port Authority Bus Terminal on Forty-Eighth Street. We hit the streets of Manhattan amidst the acrid fumes of too many busses and the smell of hot pretzels. Taxi horns blared as cars skimmed the curb, their drivers yelling obscenities in five languages. In the steamy, hazy air, we made our way through the packed streets to the Empire State Building.

From the observation deck 102 stories above the ground, we could see the mantle of hot smog that hung above the city and stretched across the Hudson far into New Jersey. We looked down to where the mouth of the Lincoln Tunnel disgorged an endless stream of vehicles and marveled that we had just been below the river. Back on the teeming street we stopped at a souvenir shop. The proprietor looked at our little group of four, all of us dark-haired, wide-eyed, and clearly ill at ease. "Come inside and look at the cameras," he invited in flawless Italian. He had sized us up and concluded that was the only possible nationality.

We returned exhausted to our mountain haven, and the girls went to spend the second week with Charlie at his house a few miles down the road. They visited dairy farms and helped milk cows. They went to a dinner with local poets, and Carla read some of her own poetry. Like most teens, she and Dezbah occasionally got bored hanging out with adults, but by and large they had a good time. When they returned home to Canyon de Chelly, the two girls described their experiences at a big family conference. They told of stopping to pray as they had been taught, even in the alien terrain of New York. Grandma Karen was proud that Carla and Dezbah turned to what they knew and remembered.

The winter of 1993 was a hard one for both Margarita and me. Our personal lives were in disarray, as her marriage finished in divorce and my two-year relationship ended. We spoke on the phone every few weeks, sharing our sadness. Margarita went to her mother for advice and in the spring she wrote me a letter offering comfort and support in the Navajo Way. Her words helped me to realize the special importance of our bonds to blood relatives. It was advice I was to remember often in the next years, as Rachel became a typical teenager and my parents grew older and my mother more infirm.

At the end of May 1993, after seven years of work, Margarita left the Park Service. Her programs had reached thousands of people each year, and her words touched some in ways that changed their lives. Groups of students from high schools and colleges across the country, as well as from local reservation schools, came into the canyon to spend time on her land as she began to work toward her dream of establishing the Canyon de Chelly Diné Institute, a nonprofit cultural and educational center to teach Navajo and non-Navajo youth to live in beauty with themselves and others.

That fall, I paid a visit to Margarita. I came simply as a friend, not an anthropologist. We hiked deep into upper Canyon del Muerto, to a spot where Douglas fir, ponderosa pine, and lush grass edged a stream that bubbled over boulders and rocks, creating small pools where catfish swam. Then we stopped at Black Rock to visit Margarita's mother, Karen, and Karen's sisters, Ellen and Janet. They were just finishing a special ceremony when we arrived.

"Yaa' at' eh," I said. Karen nodded. "*Ouu*," she said, meaning yes. I looked at her, a little puzzled. She had always greeted me with a big hug. Karen turned to Margarita and said, in Navajo. "Tell my daughter I'm sorry I can't hug her. We can't touch anyone until the ceremony is over." Margarita translated, and I nodded. "Ouu," I said.

We were there to make sure the older women had everything they needed. We had seen Karen's husband, Leonard, gathering plants, but he kept his distance during the ceremony. The three sisters seemed to be doing okay; in fact, I felt envious of their warm, easy interactions.

We had also come to ask for advice. My land in New York had recently been invaded by beavers. They were furry and cute, and ate carrots out of my hand. They also consumed ten full-sized trees each night in the fall and flooded close to seven acres of land during the summer. I loved them and enjoyed seeing them, but I was in a quandary. Which living things had the right to survive—the humans on dry, forested land, the beavers in their swamp, or the trees? What should I do?

The women listened as I told my tale and Margarita translated. Then they talked for some time among themselves. Finally Karen turned to me. "Move," she said simply. I laughed, thinking of the nomadic lifestyle of the Navajos and the many home sites they could choose between. I thought about my fifteen-year mortgage.

"I can't move," I told her. She nodded in understanding and continued. "There are sacred words. These words are so powerful that those beavers would know to move if they heard them."

"Do you know the words?" Margarita asked her mother. "No," she answered. "You'd have to get a particular medicine man to go." I shook my head. That didn't seem possible.

Karen nodded again and consulted with her sister Ellen. She turned to Margarita. "When we find ourselves in a situation where one of the four-leggeds is disrupting the balance, but we feel connected with that animal and don't want to harm it, we call in the biligáanas. We let them handle it." Margarita laughed and translated. I smiled. "I am a biligáana," I reminded her. "No, no," said Karen. "The real biligáanas. The ones who do that sort of thing."

I returned home and called the Irish-American fur trapper down the road. I hoped he was biligáana enough for the job.

In the winter of 1993–94, Margarita joined her newly founded Diné Institute with an organization called Trees for Mother Earth (TFME), which brought non-Navajo high school students into the canyon area to plant fruit trees. Margarita became canyon coordinator for TFME and traveled throughout the country to raise funds and interest schools in the project. While she was in California, we talked on the phone to set up a canyon stay for my students during the upcoming summer. She was homesick, she said, and couldn't wait to get back.

I, too, couldn't wait to get back. I had first come to Canyon de Chelly in 1990. As an anthropologist, a professional outsider, I long accepted that I was someone who thrashed about in the realities of other cultures because the one I was born into made no sense to me. In the years I knew them, Margarita and her relatives had shared much knowledge with me as we all attempted to create a balance between the logic of tradition and the relentless demands of the twenty-first century. In exchange, I showed them the life I knew and tried to portray their lives with beauty and dignity in my writing.

As this work progressed, I sent copies of the manuscript to Margarita. She read it to her family and reported their comments. They asked not to be identified by their real names, but were concerned about the Spanish-sounding names I had given them. "This is the twentieth century," said Noreen. "We want twentieth-century biligáana names like Sue or Joe." Later, they decided to stick with my original choices.

Noreen also was a stickler for accuracy. "Why didn't you include the part where Margarita went to the bathroom in the dark at the Ye'ii'bechai dance and sat down right on the prickly pear?" she asked.

Margarita commented on the manuscript and corrected those places where I had gotten something wrong. The editorial process also altered the text, and after each edit Margarita made more observations. This was an unusual process for an anthropologist, and it extended to the photographs as well. Final photo selections were made with the consent of the people pictured.

In the end, our fieldwork, and this book, developed into an experience of partnership and mutual exchange. This was something Margarita talked about when she visited my classes in New York in March 1994 and again a year later. I met her family and stayed at her houses; now she met my friends and my parents and saw the world in which I lived. When Margarita stayed at my house, sleeping in the same room where her daughter, Carla, had slept two years earlier, she felt it completed a circle. Now, though we see each other only once or twice a year, we write and call and keep that circle flowing.

During the years that Charlie and I visited the Navajos, the shape of all our lives altered, much as the shape of the canyon changes with the passage of the seasons. Rachel and Carla were becoming women, moving into an adult world. There were many new babies in the Dawson extended family, including a first daughter for Noreen. Charlie and his fiancée got married, and Margarita sent a portion of the Blessing Way to be read at their wedding. I took over the care of my parents, following the example Margarita set by taking care of her father in his last days. Both of

Karen with babies Margaret and Isaiah on cradleboards.

us faced changes in our lives and in our relationships with those who meant the most to us. We still asked each other for advice, acknowledging that our different worlds have provided us with diverse and valuable skills that we can use to cross between them.

Summer 2007

Almost three years later, in 1997, Charlie and I flew into Albuquerque during an October weekend when light and color and climate conspired to make me contemplate a permanent change of residence. We rented the usual Geo Metro and drove to the School of American Research (SAR) Press in Santa Fe to pick up several cases of the newly released, original edition of *Crossing Between Worlds*. It was time to make good on our promise of a copy for each person or family appearing in the text. This was important to us, as we were well aware that the track record for photographers and ethnographers working in Navajo Country has not been good. In fact, some of Charlie's best images never made it to publication, though we did bring prints back to the family.

"Edward Curtis photographed my family when he was out here," said an angry and protective son, referring to one of the images in Curtis'

1903 *Vanishing Indian* series. "He never paid us. Ansel Adams photographed my mother in the 1950s, and he never paid us." He paused and looked Charlie in the eye. "And you don't have enough money to pay us to use my mother's photograph."

Other, more candid shots were left out of the original version of the book for lighter reasons. "Can you crop this at my chest, so I look thinner?" asked Margarita's sister, referring to a playful photo of her at Black Rock in the clown mask next to Karen.

On the day scheduled for book distribution, Margarita gathered family and friends in her Tsaile home. We spent the day driving up and down the two rims, dropping off copies at the homes of many of the elderlies who had been part of our interviews. Now, the compact living-dining area of Margarita's two-bedroom BIA house began to fill. She flitted back and forth between her guests and the large fry pans filled with hot Crisco, preparing a batch of Navajo tacos.

A group of grandmas in their velveteen best flipped through copies of the book, pointing at each other's photos and smiling with approval. They talked among themselves, relaxed and animated, and finally, Margarita translated. "They say that they really like the way the book came out, but next time, for the next book, they'd like to dress up in the old way, and get the wagons out, and take pictures of how things used to be."

I shook my head and we rolled our eyes at each other. We tried so hard to represent Navajo life as it was becoming, to capture and preserve a document for the young people to have. This was Aunt Ellen's intent when she finally signed her photo release, as life was changing at such an incredible pace.

Our promise to come back and photograph, at the very least, a calendar of images of that remembered way of canyon life with the grandmas has never been fulfilled. The cycle of life is just that, a continuing and unchoreographed process. We grow into our unfolding roles, new members are born into our family communities, and others pass on. There are many images absent from this edition of *Crossing Between Worlds*. As we made the final selections—each of us choosing our favorite twenty—I asked Margarita if we could use the photos of those no longer with us, respecting the custom of not showing photos or making direct reference to those who we have lost. She thought for a moment and then, in true Navajo fashion, said, "I'll have to ask my mother." Karen's response was also very much in Navajo tradition. "We should not think about those sad moments or have pictures that remind us of them. This book is about looking ahead."

Like many of the elderlies of Margarita's family, my mom, blessedly, passed over in 1998, and Dad was not far behind her. He had no expansive cadre of daughters surrounding him as Margarita's family does—

only one daughter. I guess it got pretty lonely for him. With their passing, Karen, my Navajo mom, reminded me of the great web of Navajo kinship. She gave me an enveloping hug.

"My daughter has no mother," she said. "I have no sister." We both cried for our loss.

Karen's concern for me reflected another obligation. As my only surviving elder relative, she felt it her duty to help me find a mate. There was always someone in the next canyon, recently widowed, with a good piece of land, and a big tractor, who was suggested as a possibility. Marriage is about alliance.

Finally, in 2001, I called Margarita to say I was coming to visit with an academic colleague of mine, Duncan Earle. Karen was delighted. She decided he was a prospective mate—possible family—and got ready. Part of the Diné marriage custom involves the man butchering a sheep for his mother-in-law to show he has the adequate skills to keep his prospective family going. Karen waited for us at Black Rock, knife in hand. "The sheep's over there," she told Duncan, pointing with her lower lip toward the corral behind the house. We were sorry to disappoint her.

In 1999, I moved from my beloved Oneonta, grey and cold as it sometimes was, to become chairperson of the Department of Anthropology at Wake Forest University in North Carolina. By then, my Oneonta students had constructed "New York Fence" along the far side of Margarita's gradually developing farm near the junction. Under the direction of her new husband, Timothy Connelly—a big Navajo with an Irish name, a broad grin, and an even broader sense of humor—the students cut and set poles, and loved every minute of it. In 2001, a combined group from Duncan's University of Texas in El Paso and Wake Forest added "North Carolina Fence."

At Canyon de Chelly National Monument, another natural cycle was moving full circle, this time concerning policy related to soil conservation. In the 1930s, during the dustbowl era of drought and erosion, the management teams of the newly created national monument followed current wisdom and planted tamarisk and Russian olives along the edge of the wash. Seventy years later, when Tim and Margarita and the students began building North Carolina fence, Tim contemplated ways to wreak death and destruction on the thick border of trees. They drank up the water that should have been available to nurture newly planted corn and reduced the amount of land available for farming. By 2005, the Park Service had also reached the limits of tolerance for the previous century's solution to an ecological problem. Concluding an environmental assessment on how to manage the two aggressive species, the current park superintendent, who was the monument archaeologist when Margarita and I were rangers, determined there were five alternatives:

- a no-action alternative, which required no control actions for tamarisk or Russian olive;
- the preferred alternative A, to test and implement, as appropriate, a variety of control treatments applicable for use in the park, including: stump cutting with direct herbicide application, low-volume basal spray, heavy equipment with rotor mounted tree shredder, and whole tree removal with heavy equipment;
- an additional alternative B stump cutting and direct herbicide application only (including low- volume basal spraying)—the environmentally preferred solution;
- an additional alternative C, mechanical removal with heavy equipment with rotor mounted tree shredder only; and
- an additional alternative D, whole tree removal with heavy equipment only.

When I returned to visit Margarita and Tim in 2006, Tim waved his arm and pursed his lips in a subtle smile. "What's different?" he asked me. I looked around the farm, staring across the wash at the russet-colored canyon walls below the south rim, toward the place where the track known as "Woman Trail" came over the edge. What was different? Then it dawned on me. I could see the other side of the wash. The huge wall of olives and tamarisk was gone.

"We'll see next season if we get more water to the corn and fruit trees," he said. I was a bit more skeptical. They'd used alternative A at their farm. "Wonder how long they'll stay gone?" I mused.

That particular abatement program, a solution to a problem that had once seemed to be the solution to a problem, reminded Margarita of yet another abatement process they endured a few years earlier. Reservation housing is not always the best project proposed; it is more often the most economical of the contracts considered by the BIA and the federal government. Margarita and Tim's Tsaile complex, where we stayed on many occasions, and celebrated the original publication of the book in 1997, consisted of solidly built, four-room units that, at first glance, seemed sound. But in 2001, residents were notified they had to move out. The homes were about to be stripped of asbestos, lead, and other potentially lethal minerals that might have entered the walls, cement, insulation, and flooring. Once again, science had taken a second look at previously acceptable practice.

"They told us it would take six months, a year, and that we could move to Phoenix or Albuquerque at the government's expense if we wanted to. Most of the residents did. But we told them, we have a tour business, and it's here in the canyon. We want to stay on the peninsula, at DezAh."

DezAh was still an unimproved homesite, without electricity, water, or phone. To run their growing business, Margarita and Tim needed computer access, with Internet, so they could maintain their Web site and monitor reservations for stays at the junction farm. Unable to convince the pair that they would be happier in an apartment in Tucson, the government provided a generator and cell phone Internet access. They paid for gas to get Tim back and forth into the mountains, an eighty-mile round trip, to transport wood and water. What they would not pay for was a larger water tank, roughly equal to the cost of gas for one trip to haul water.

The couple remained on the peninsula for almost a year while the homes in their complex were stripped to only the steel framing. When it was all over, the expanse of the living room and dining area seemed a lit-

Karen with Isaiah and Margaret, pictured on page 107 in their cradleboards, at age 15 in 2007.

tle more open, and the carpets were new. The entrance to the house was in a slightly different location. Tim was philosophical. "Took them a year to move the door," he noted.

In 2005, Charlie made exhibition-sized prints of some of the *Crossing Between Worlds* images. The exhibit opened in Oneonta, then moved to the Guilford Native American Center in Greensboro, North Carolina, and finally to the Museum of Anthropology at Wake Forest University. Margarita and Tim flew to North Carolina, as did Charlie, and we held a series of cultural events on the Wake Forest campus. In the tiny kitchen attached to the anthropology department, we cooked fry bread and made Navajo tacos. Margarita explained Diné religious philosophy. My students tried once again to explain the mixed pagan-Christian symbolism of Easter.

By the time of this visit, yet another turn in time's cycle had occurred. Margarita and I found ourselves musing about the amount of grey dancing though our hair. She wondered why it was that the new generation of Navajo elders was so much greyer than her mom's cohort. "Maybe it's because we use so many chemical shampoos on our hair. Nobody uses yucca root any more," she said. "Maybe it's because people aren't out in the sun as much, and perhaps hair responds the way skin does," I added. Margarita laughed. "I think it's stress," she said, half in jest and half in contemplation.

We were quiet for a few moments, thinking of our families. The four young teens who frolicked in the rain at my Oneonta farm were now young women. Each of them faced the prospect of trying to find a balance in the world of peers and change and risk that surrounds young people in the twenty-first century. Carla and Dezbah, in addition, were also enveloped in the difficult cultural milieu of the reservation. The lives of all four reminded me of a traffic light: sometimes green, sometimes glaring red; at others, a caution-filled yellow. They grew, left home, came home, got lost. Some got found. Some are still wandering.

Margarita and I both moved into the venerable Navajo realm of grandma. During the North Carolina trip, we traveled to the coast and visited my two-year-old granddaughter, the child of Elanor, my oldest. For Margarita, the grandma role was a by-product of the Navajo kinship system, where the child of your sister is also your daughter, and her children become your grandchildren. As part of the same extended family, we considered all of the grandkids to be ours. Her family was wide and welcoming, and it was good to be a part of it. My daughter enjoyed opening her coastal home to our Diné branch.

As I drove my Subaru wagon onto the Fort Fisher-Southport car ferry on the North Carolina coast, Margarita was dubious. She smiled broadly. "My Mom, Karen, is not going to believe this," she said. Even as Margarita became an emerging elder, Karen remained the family matriarch. In

Karen on cell phone, 2007.

Karen and Leonard, 2007.

her mid eighties, she was still weaving, though she often complained that she could no longer see well enough to complete a rug.

Her daughter Lora was skeptical. Driving home one day from basketball practice with her now teenaged son, Isaiah, one of the babies Karen held in a cradleboard on the cover of the original edition of *Crossing Between Worlds,* she passed Karen, who was shopping at Basha's, and failed to make a stop. "I saw you drove by," Karen told her later. So much for failing vision.

Karen's eyesight had been the topic of deep reflection for the family a few years previous. With cataracts obscuring her ability to work and weave and walk in the canyon, the doctors at the IHS clinic proposed surgery. There was some talk of tissue transplant, which, in essence, meant putting a portion of someone who was dead into your body. Whether this was the case or not, surgery was a difficult decision for those living in the Navajo Way, even though Karen wanted to be able to see. Margarita called me and explained. "It's gonna take some pretty big ceremonies," she told me, to make this okay with the Holy People. "We're starting next week." I sent my contribution.

Lora finished her education and became a teacher, returning to Tsaile to teach about both Navajo culture and the world outside of the reservation's borders. In the summer of 2006, she traveled to France with a group of young people, including her own son and Everett, who'd journeyed to Japan years before. Caroline Tso also returned to school, completed a degree in anthropology, and took a job as an archaeologist for the Park Service.

Education was important as well for my daughter Rachel, the little girl whose penchant for horses brought me to Canyon de Chelly. In 2007, she received a BSN, her license as a registered nurse, and moved to the city of Seattle. Like Margarita and Tim, she still loves horses.

Recently, I visited the junction farm with an acquaintance of mine. An Australian aborigine, she dreamed of meeting her counterparts in the U.S., so we traveled to Canyon de Chelly and spent the night in the quiet peace below the towering walls of the junction farm. She and Margarita compared experiences, and the world got a little smaller.

Margarita's Reflections: July 2007

One day I woke up with some grey hair and I thought I grew so old in one day like my 83-year-old grandmother—it can't be! I'm going to go to a Song and Dance to find a Navajo (Diné) Man that isn't related to me to spend the rest of my life with. Well, I had to make one more stop to get some firewood for my aunt who lived by herself at DezAh (Canyon

Point). After one of my twelve sisters and I finished loading up the pickup truck with wood, we decided to stop for some water to drink out of the DezAh windmill tank. While we were there, we heard a very noisy truck. It seemed like the whole canyons, Canyon del Muerto and Canyon de Chelly, were going to crumble down. If that had happened our canyon would have been bigger than Grand Canyon.

As we stood, sincerely confused, to see who was speeding down the dirt road, we could only see a giant string of dust on the one and only four-season peninsula dirt road. We were hearing the pickup truck but we still didn't see it! To our surprise, it quickly appeared only about fifty feet away from us. We thought that dusty, rusty truck was never going to stop. Brakes and smoke started to burn out from that truck when out of that almost white, dusty Ford came my nephew J.R. He was followed by friends, about ten dusty brown Indians; a few were tall, more were fat, two were skinny, some were short. Our nephew was almost the same age as us; he was older than some of my younger sisters. So, we both immediately said, "We got to go, we don't want to be where my crazy nephew and his crazy friends are, nope, nope, nope."

As we headed for our Chevy truck, one of my nephew's buddies followed us and he plied us with smart remarks. "Who in the world loaded that eyelash wood? You don't use that kind of firewood unless you want to freeze. No one wants ashes; they'd rather have big red charcoal." I immediately said, "Save your breath. We don't see *you* working. You don't even have a sharp tool in your hands, so just go away."

After a few lousy communications, I can't believe I actually asked Tim, my nephew's good buddy, to help us unload the wood for my aunt. When we were unloading the wood, he finally agreed that some wood was heavy. From that moment my life changed. I never saw it coming until something flew in my heart—fire, sparks—and we started talking like we've never talked before. I guess you could say I listened to my elders.

At the end of the day, Tim and I became good friends and I decided to take our relatives' advice. I heard my four aunts often say, "Tim is a good, hard-working Diné man. He fixes fences, makes good firewood, is a good deer hunter, and has a job. One of you single young women should marry Tim." We all said, "Yuk, he only listens to Jimmy Horton on his radio." But within one year we were married. We both took life serious from that moment on. He had no choice but to leave his home and live with me and take care of the *kin ya aanii* land. But there was one more last problem to show Tim, and that was the canyon life.

"Where is the farm?" he said as he stood looking over *Yei' bi cheii'* trail at the land below. Canyon farm had overgrown with weeds and we couldn't even see the old shade house. I told him if he wanted to make our marriage strong he had to improve the farm at Canyon de Chelly, too. We both found the canyon to be hard, but it also gave us serenity and support in so many ways. We started a hiking and overnight camping tour company and that opportunity let us meet wonderful people. Most of them became good friends, we all learned many different cultures from each other.

When I worked as a Park Ranger at Canyon de Chelly National Monument, I felt like a horse with hobbles; I couldn't do very much then. Now, our lives have changed just being tour guides. I could not have ever imagined that was possible. I actually learned to bake a cake from a card-board box. I learned how to cook fish. I had my fresh salmon fish at Canyon de Chelly. I learned that you can live in a tent for two weeks. I learned that there were actually hiking boots. I learned chocolate is made from nuts and that some cars run by McDonald French fries. I learned that people can stop work and come out to Canyon de Chelly for relaxation. Wow! I thought the canyon was only for work and some play.

I am learning so much! It feels like I'm going to a private school, and of course with great teachers. They share their lives, where they work, and what type of foods they eat, how and when they sleep, why they don't care too much for the government. All these years I thought they were all working for the government! It was a big relief for me. I guess that is why I can communicate with biligáana better now.

One big difference is there are only about three or, at the most, four people in their family. My grandmother used to say, "Have lots of family. If you do, you will always be happy and strong."

Most of the time I am happy but I don't know about being strong. Physically, I am not strong but I guess I can't take no for an answer wisely. So, I guess we all live the way the Holy People want us to live. I know that most of the people that come to our home are very friendly and a great help. From 1984 to now, all the biligáanas I met have been just wonderful. Some of them became very close friends and some are like family. When our guests came to tour, some worked on fences, some dug out a pit for water so Marie's sheep could drink water. Some planted fruit trees and corn, some put mud on the hogan and most of them left our home with great love and respect for the Diné and the land, Canyon de Chelly.

One big change in our life is that we were given a chance to raise a grandson, Deon. He is our grandson by one of my dear nieces and she's the daughter of one of my sisters. Deon is now five years old, but we had Deon in our home at DezAh when he was six months. Deon and my daughter Carla keep us grounded. They are always in our prayers and heart. Carla is on her own these days. She sometimes stops by at Tsaile and babysits for us. She is still searching for her destiny gracefully. But when she doesn't call, that's when we worry.

Now, I am a parent all over again and Tim has been so patient and great with his grandson, who he treats like his own son. Tim and Deon

Top left: Margarita and Tim.
Top right: Grandson Deon.
Bottom: Tim and Margarita with their horses.

are like a pair of moccasins. They already have traveled to so many places together. They both love their five horses, DeChelly, Dawn, Star, Rainbow, and Shirley. The family does trail rides from Canyon de Chelly to Chuska Mountains or Tec Nos Pos every summer and Deon rides his favorite horse, DeChelly. They also sometimes ride their horses in a summer ceremony, the Enemy Way—Ni' daah.

We (Deon, Tim and I) also rode airplanes to Portland, Oregon, to visit our friends Dr. Tori Hudson and Dee Packard, and to San Francisco to visit more special friends: Emery and Chris, Tim Fox, and David and Barbara Lazarony. At these places I learned to soak in a hot bubbly tub called a hot tub. I just love hot tubs. Tim has a hard time getting us out of that amazing experience. Deon also loves this tub.

Sometimes my mom asks me what I do when I travel. Oh boy, I have a hard time explaining about things, I told her that you sit in a hot tub half naked and the bubbles grab and massage your skin. She responded, and said, "Why go through all that trouble; just walk to the canyon rim after the rain and sit in a pot hole." Tim has a great sense of humor. He says, "You better get out of that hot tub or else it's going to turn into 'Mutton Stew.'" He only says that because I eat a lot of mutton stew and fry bread.

Margarita (Summer, 2007)

So far, my life has been incredibly blessed by the Holy People. There have been a few struggles, but it's always been replaced by more of the positive outcomes. There were a few hardships for the family, but my elders had done a good job explaining about birth and death to me at an early age.

When someone passes on into their spiritual world, you only cry for four days in your home; that is beginning to be very tough to do now. I try to continue to communicate with the air, water, fire and the soil after four days of our loss. Our elders taught us that all our relatives that pass on are the rain drops, flowers, mountains, rocks, trees, and animals so we must continue to talk to them with love and respect. Sometimes it is hard to make that connection when there are government policies tangled around nature. It is also hard to do that because a lot of our own people do not speak the Diné language and practice the culture anymore. Making positive connections with Mother Earth and Father Sky as our ancestors taught us are practices slowly fading away.

Well, with all this, I didn't so much grow up but I grew with many different kinds of experiences, some good and some not so good. Many of my elders that are in the book, *Crossing Between Worlds,* passed on and some were my young relatives. Some were close relatives to my dear friends in North Carolina, Portland, Palo Alto, and Phoenix. They traveled into their spiritual journeys. Before they left, they left a seed—a seed that will never end. That is why we are still here in the Fifth World.

The most painful and memorable was my Aunt Ellen passing, only because she took with her most of the Canyon de Chelly Diné cultural ways of life. My world stood empty that cold December. The government and the mission say she was born on December 26; she passed on December 23. Some Canyon de Chelly walls have fallen for her and some trees and animals left with her. The weather was harsh that year. Ellen was the oldest true traditional Diné woman. When she lived, everyone stopped their daily chores when she approached. Ellen's words were powerful and sometimes strict. Whenever and whatever words came out of her mouth were usually lessons. Her old ways of wisdom died that day, but her lessons are now becoming clearer. She has been my greatest teacher.

We were driving out of the muddy canyon and my mind drifted off to thinking about how many times we went out and in from the canyon. And they are all always different. I remember one summer dragging out a donkey with our truck; the donkey just couldn't stay away from our mares. There was another time we were speeding up the very deep sandy road trying to not get stuck when our family friend and in-law, Scott, tried to hang on to the truck but he fell out of the truck. It was a good thing he landed on the soft sand; he's okay. There was also a time when we got caught in a flash flood. My husband was driving and he was still in the truck when about ten feet of water just came gushing down the canyon. It took the truck and it almost turned over. That was very scary. We lost our truck, but kept my husband. The next spring we managed to get another truck, and guess where we drove it to? Yes, back to the canyon. Sometimes there is no other way of life but to keep going back to your canyon life.

There were also a lot of happy times; the canyon is where I first drove a tractor. I walked to work and school from Ye' bi cheii Trail. We ran with the ki' nal daa during Ki' nal daa ceremony to White Sands trail and back to our home. When I was a little girl I don't know how many times I saw my moccasins float away. During monsoon rain the muddy water always took my shoes from me. We also rode our horses in and out of the canyon and I don't know how many times we walked the canyons. Canyon life gives you adventures, it brings you unforgettable experiences.

With this in mind, we decided to share the canyon life with people— people searching for dirt road path experiences at Canyon de Chelly. We named these experiences, "*Footpath Journeys of Canyon de Chelly*". It is our fourteenth year of doing hiking and camping tours. It is not a job for us; it's sharing our culture with many other cultures. It's a rare experience; sometimes people don't want to leave our home after their tour with us, mostly everyone has tears in their eyes when they are departing, because we all have become great friends. We—my family and I—also get watery eyes and sometimes we cry. They loved the experiences and they don't want it to end.

Through time we were able to get a computer, telephone, and cell phone for more connections for possible visits. We enjoy and treasure what we offer; it's a rare, delicate and important experience we do for people. My elderly people always said, "If you have lots of relatives visiting you, you will never be lonely."

Sometimes people become like families and they continue to come back. There has been a lot of friendship that was made from this experience. The people get a chance to come in to our home, our hogan; we laugh, share stories and eat together. Everyday we walk to many different beautiful places in the canyon. We see animal people, bird people, plant people, and rock people as we walk and we share ancient stories and they began to understand why we consider everything as alive and that we all are connected. Everyone shares a story of their culture, as the days turn into night we are connecting bridges between many cultures.

Every day is always a new experience. People learn about how they connect positively with Mother Earth and Father Sky and everything around them. During their stay, everyone becomes a family. Believing in Mother Earth and Father Sky, we believe our environment is so valuable and precious that we do not offer jeep tours. Our vision is to reach more people to help them to understand and respect nature and each other's culture so the world we live in can be more safe, in happiness and beauty.

One other goal we pray for is sharing the canyon life with our own youth. It's a shame today; some of our youth are forgetting their stories, culture, history, language, and relatives. Maybe if we reach the students, they might get a chance to relearn their stories, sleep in our traditional hogan, build cooking fires, and be able to eat traditional foods. Then they will also make many travels from their sacred canyon lands. We would like that all the students enter the canyon with an open mind and heart to learn of the sacredness of the canyon, not just for recreation.

So much has been accomplished as we offer these amazing journeys. First we completed our traditional home, the hogan. We planted about fifteen fruit trees and they are doing well. We now have water catchments for our animals. A relative plows our field every year. We can plant corn and squash. We built structures, sun showers, an outside kitchen, out-houses, and storage.

My husband is making another hogan at Black Rock. One of theses days we will see the canyon resident's farms fill with fruits and vegetables. Diné people will be working with their fields, like a long time ago. There may be less government handouts. Last but not least, some state funding and a private party (Dr. Tori Hudson) are building a solar water pump for irrigation in our home. My eyes will be filling with happiness tears. I am so fortunate to have chosen to stay with the land—my ancestral land at Canyon de Chelly. I am so glad my people kept the land, especially through times of hardships. It is amazing to see all different cultures coming to help us sustain our livelihood. Many of the people bring positive energy all the time. My mother, grandmother, and her grandmother say, "Live today, not the future or the past. Always have positive thoughts. Never have negative thoughts; they will only harm you."

That is why we welcome all people that are able to come, to come and be part of our home, family, and friends. You have to understand that you live today not in the past and not in the future. You have to have a good understanding with what you have—your family, loved ones, ani-mals, home. Learn to respect and adapt to them with what you learned. Remember, everything comes from Mother Earth and Father Sky. Work with what may work today. You can't have too much of something; it's not so good. And you can't have too little; it may not meet a certain stan-dard. You have to almost juggle to feel a balance.

Anthropologists go into the field to learn about relationships, to live in the physical and spiritual fabric of someone else's life. In the past, when the research was over, we just left, returning to our own homes and lives. The months we spent away were contained in small spiral note-books filled with scribbled thoughts and observations, or in colored blan-kets displayed on our walls. We wrote our ethnographies and thought fondly of the lengthy respite from academic routine. But in the last decade, anthropologists have begun to share not just ethnographic voice but also their royalties and book prizes as well. We have come to realize that learning is an exchange; fieldwork is an ongoing commitment. Sur-rounded by the familiar trappings of our own lives, we realize we have been changed by the experience, as have our partners and colleagues in the communities we seek to understand. It's as if we all find ourselves

standing in a funhouse hall of mirrors: we are ourselves, reflected in the lives of others, reflected in our own lives, in theirs, ours, theirs. . . .

The legacy of this experience called fieldwork is change—both subtle and obvious—for everyone involved. Its challenge is not just to see and know other people, but to juggle for a meaningful balance, learning from the reflecting pool of each other's realities, to gain a fuller understanding of what it is to be human. To that understanding, Margarita offers a short prayer:

> Beauty from Mother Earth, Beauty from Father Sky, I am your child, I am your little one, and may there be beauty all around me. Thank you for making me who I am, thank you for my forefathers for who they are, my children for who they are. All the Holy People, bless me with everything around me, bless the canyon, bless my relatives, and bless all my friends. Bless all the people and all my friend's journeys as they walk Canyon de Chelly and Canyon del Muerto. A' yee' hei', May there be beauty from all directions, it has become beauty again.

Opposite page: Dog Rock at sunset.

Sources

The Navajo are the largest Native American nation in the United States, and the body of scholarly and popular literature on them is substantial. In writing this book, I relied heavily on works produced by Navajos. Such sources supplement classic works and specialized texts by anthropologists and historians working in Navajo studies. Each of these will direct the interested reader to additional sources.

General sources exclusively about the Navajos are Goodman (1982), Iverson (1983, 1990), Kluckhohn and Leighton (1951), and Underhill (1956). Iverson and Roessel (2002) provide a comprehensive history, accompanied by an excellent bibliography of further readings. An additional comprehensive bibliography appears in Bahr (1999). Other works about Southwestern peoples with substantive sections on the Navajo are Ortiz (1983), Spicer (1962), and Trimble (1993). For general information about Southwestern archaeology, see Cordell (1997) and Martin and Plog (1973).

Prologue: Finding the Trail

An administrative history of Canyon de Chelly National Monument can be found in Brugge and Wilson (1976).

Some of the general problems facing resident or indigenous peoples in protected areas and national parks are discussed in Brechin and West (1990), Crespi (1991), *Cultural Survival Quarterly* (1985), Fletcher (1990), Rao and Geisler (1990), Sadler (1989), Saunders (1990), West (1991), and Zube and Busch (1990). An overview of park-resident relationships at Canyon de Chelly can be found in Simonelli (1992). "Margarita Dawson" tells her own story in Johnson (1992). Additional memoirs of Canyon de Chelly appear in Moore (2004) and Cumming (2006).

Chapter 1: Facing East

The shoe game is described in Yazzie (1971).

Kunitz and Levy (1991) describe the transition from family care to institutional care for the elderly that has begun to take place among the Navajos.

For a comprehensive survey of rock art and prehistory in Canyon de Chelly, see Grant (1978); for a discussion of design elements in Four Corners rock art, see Barnes (1982). Polly Schaafsma has published widely on Southwestern rock art; an overview can be found in Schaafsma (1980). Will Tsossie of the Chinle Public Schools told the story of rock art and the Holy People during the 1990 Canyon de Chelly ranger orientation. Navajo history is recounted in Yazzie (1971); see also Zolbrod (1984). Portions of the story appear in Bingham and Bingham (1982). A history of Canyon de Chelly place names and trails appears in Jeet (2000).

For more about Earl Morris and early archaeology at Canyon de Chelly, see Lister and Lister (1968). A photographic review of Morris's career in archaeology is found in Lange and Leonard (1985). For reminiscences about the early days of archaeology in the Southwest, see Judd (1968) and Snead (2004).

Cordell (1997) is a reliable source for information about Southwestern archaeological sequences and reports the naming of the Anasazi. Descriptions of the Morris expeditions in Canyon de Chelly appear in Ann Axtell Morris (1934).

For information concerning Navajo history prior to 1680, see Hogan (1989). Acrey (1988) is a comprehensive history of the Navajos, while McNitt (1972) concentrates on military interactions. Thompson (1976) focuses on the Bosque Redondo period; oral histories of that period can be found in Roessel (1973).

Chapter 2: Blue Sky Morning

For a discussion of witchcraft in Navajo culture, see Kluckhohn (1967) and Simmons (1974:135–136).

Beck, Walters, and Francisco (1992) have compiled a fine volume explaining Native American religion, including sections on Navajo beliefs and ceremonies; see especially 267–289. See also Zolbrod (1984), Locke (1990), and Yazzie (1971).

Works concerning economic development on the reservation include Ortiz (1980) and Reno (1981); see also Acrey (1988). Concerning energy development, see Chamberlain (2000) and Eachstaedt (1994). Statistics on Navajo development can be found in Navajo Nation (1988). For crafts in particular, see Trahant (1996).

Acrey (1988) summarizes education and the history of school systems on the reservation through the 1960s; continuing dialogue on Native Americans and education takes place in each issue of the quarterly journal, *Winds of Change: American Indian Education and Opportunity.* See also Hyer (1990) and Reynher et al. (2000). An examination of the experiences of a Navajo woman with higher education appears in Evans (1993). Aberle (1989) looks at the relationship between education, work, and gender. Statistics on Navajo education can be found in Navajo Nation (1988).

See Schoepfle et al. (1983) concerning Navajo use of alcohol. See also Schwarz (2001) and Alvord and Van Pelt (1999) for more on this and health issues in general.

Acrey (1988) provides a historical summary of Navajo–livestock relationships; for greater detail see Bailey (1980), Boyce (1974), Henderson (1989), Johnson and Roessel (1974), and Trimble (1993). For Canyon de Chelly, see Andrews (1998). See McNitt (1962) and Federal Trade Commission (1973) for a history of traders and trading posts on the Navajo Reservation.

Excellent photographs of White House Ruin at the turn of the century appear in McLuhan (1985).

Begay (1983) gives a comprehensive description of Kinaalda; see also Yazzie (1971:31–35). Concerning Navajo women, see McCullough-Brabson and Help (2001) and Niethammer (2001).

For a version of the story of Spider Woman, see Locke (1990:199). Navajo origins in general are covered in Levy (1998) Linford (2000), and Towner (1996).

Chapter 3: Warm Golden Wind

Materials for interpretation at Canyon de Chelly are presented in Moffett (1981) and in Hunter and King (1990). Goldman (1990) and Weber (1990) discuss interpretation and Native Americans.

For a review of back-country management proposals at Canyon de Chelly, see National Park Service, Navajo Nation, and BIA (1990). The excavations at Antelope House are described in Morris (1986).

The rationale behind recent archaeology at Canyon de Chelly was explained to me by Scott Travis, National Park Service archaeologist at Canyon de Chelly. For a look at current perspectives on archaeological research, see Graves (1994).

The notion of "sacred" is discussed in Beck, Walters, and Francisco (1992:1–36) and Kelley and Frances (1994). Canyon de Chelly's statement concerning the sacred first appeared in National Park Service (1991).

For a discussion of agriculture in Canyon de Chelly, see Stoker (1990) and especially Andrews (1985; 1998).

A complete survey of sandpainting can be found in Parezo (1983). See also Griffen Pierce (1992).

Books about Navajo weaving are plentiful. An early history appears in Amsden (1964) and a historical analysis in Kent (1985); see also Dutton (1961), Rodee (1995) and McCloskey (2002). Both Bennett (1974) and Reichard (1968) link weaving to Navajo sacred traditions, as does Zolbrod and Willink (1996).

Beck, Walters, and Francisco (1992) give an overview of Navajo ceremonial "ways." Medicine man Albert Yazzie discussed the loss of ceremonial knowledge in a talk during Canyon de Chelly's interpretive orientation in 1990.

Chapter 4: Sleeping Thunder

Grant (1978) describes Hopi seasonal occupation of the de Chelly area.

The boarding school era is described in Acrey (1988) and especially in Hyer (1990).

Acrey (1988) summarizes Navajo political history; Deloria and Lytle (1984) address the question of Native American sovereignty. Deloria (1991) presents a number of philosophical essays concerning Native American education. Helsley and Kawano (2001) provide a portrait of the Navajo nation today.

Roessel (1981) discusses the importance of children to Navajo mothers in her larger discussion of women in Navajo society; see also Lamphere (1977).

Issues of jurisdiction on the Navajo Reservation were explained to me by Reed Riner and David Zimmerman, both of the Department of Anthropology, Northern Arizona University.

For statistics on Navajo birth rates, see Indian Health Service (1990) and Navajo Nation (1988); see also Aberle (1989) for a discussion of the relationship between wage labor, modernization, and family size. Lamphere (1989) focuses on wage labor and Navajo women. The history of family planning and abortion is summarized in Temkin-Greener et al. (1981). Roessel (1981) discusses the importance of children to the Navajo family. Broudy and May (1983) and Kunitz (1983) address the demographic and epidemiological transition among the Navajos.

For an excellent discussion of the peyote religion among the Navajos, as well as an overview of Navajo religious philosophy, see Aberle (1991); see also Beck, Walters, and Francisco (1992:225–244). Concerning Navajo women and ceremony, see Schwarz (2003).

Epilogue: Reflecting Pools

Photos of Canyon de Chelly residents appear in Curtis et al. (2000) and Adams and Stillman (2007), among others. A discussion of the relationship between photography and Native Americans appears in Doty, Mudge, and Benally (2002) and Faris (1997). Analyses of concerns related to health and healing appear in Schwarz (2003; 2008) and Davies (2001). Park Service plans for environmental management at Canyon de Chelly can be found in Travis (2005). Issues of cultural continuity and change are addressed in House (2002) and O'Neill (2005); see also Carmean (2002). Concerning Native American grandmas, see Schweitzer (1999).

References

Aberle, David
> 1991 *The Peyote Religion among the Navajo.* 2nd ed. Norman: University of Oklahoma Press.
> 1989 Education, Work, Gender and Residence: Black Mesa Navajos in the 1960s. *Journal of Anthropological Research* 45(4):405–430.

Acrey, Bill P.
> 1988 *Navajo History: The Land and the People.* Shiprock, NM: Department of Curriculum Materials Development, Central Consolidated School District No. 22.

Adams, Ansel and Andrea Stillman
> 2007 *Ansel Adams: 400 Photographs.* New York: Bulfinch Press.

Alvord, Lori Arviso, with Elizabeth Cohen Van Pelt.
> 1999 *The Scalpel and the Silver Bear: The First Navajo Woman Surgeon Combines Western Medicine with Traditional Healing.* New York: Bantam.

Ambler, Maryjane
> 1990 *Breaking the Iron Bonds: Indian Control of Energy Development.* Lawrence: University Press of Kansas.

Amsden, Charles A.
> 1964 *Navajo Weaving: Its Technique and History.* 1934. Reprint, Santa Ana, CA: The Fine Arts Press.

Andrews, Tracy J.
> 1985 *Descent, Land Use, and Inheritance: Navajo Land Tenure Patterns in Canyon de Chelly and Canyon del Muerto.* Ph.D. dissertation, University of Arizona, Tucson.
> 1998 Crops, Cattle, and Capital: Agrarian Political Ecology in Canyons de Chelly and del Muerto. *American Indian Culture and Research Journal* 22(3):31–78.
> 1994 A Family History of Alcohol Use, In *Drinking Careers: A Twenty-five Year Study of Three Navajo Populations*, S. Kunitz and J. Levy, eds. New Haven: Yale University Press.

Bahr, Howard.
> 1999 *Diné Bibliography to the 1990s: A Companion to Navajo Tribal Bibliography of 1969.* Lanham, MD: Scarecrow Press.

Bailey, Garrick and Roberta Glenn Bailey
> 1986 *A History of The Navajos: The Reservation Years.* Santa Fe: School of American Research Press

Bailey, Lynn
    1980 *If You Take My Sheep: The Evolution and Conflicts of Navajo Pastoralism, 1630–1868.* Pasadena, CA: Westernlore Publications.
Barnes, F. A.
    1982 *Canyon Country Prehistoric Rock Art.* Salt Lake City: Wasatch Publishers.
Beck, Peggy V., Anna Lee Walters, and Nia Francisco
    1992 *The Sacred: Ways of Knowledge, Sources of Life.* Tsaile, AZ: Navajo Community College Press.
Begay, Shirley M.
    1983 *Kinaalda: A Navajo Puberty Ceremony.* Rough Rock, AZ: Navajo Curriculum Center, Rough Rock Demonstration School.
Bennett, Noel
    1974 *The Weaver's Pathway: A Clarification of the "Spirit Trail" in Navajo Weaving.* Flagstaff, AZ: Northland Press.
Bingham, Sam and Janet Bingham, eds.
    1982 *Between Sacred Mountains: Navajo Stories and Lessons from the Land.* Tucson: Sun Tracks and the University of Arizona Press.
Boyce, George A.
    1974 *When Navajos Had Too Many Sheep: The 1940s.* San Francisco: The Indian Historian Press.
Brechin, S. R. and P. C. West
    1990 Protected Areas, Resident Peoples and Sustainable Conservation: The Need to Link Top Down with Bottom Up. *Society and Natural Resources* 3:77–79.
Broudy, D., and P. A. May
    1983 Demographic and Epidemiologic Transition among the Navajos. *Sociobiology* 30(1).
Brugge, D., and R. Wilson
    1976 *Administrative History of Canyon de Chelly National Monument, Arizona.* Washington, DC: Government Printing Office.
Carmean, Kelli
    2002 *Spider Woman Walks This Land: Traditional Cultural Properties and the Navajo Nation.* Walnut Creek, CA: Alta Mira
Cordell, Linda S.
    1997 *Archaeology of the Southwest.* 2nd Edition. Orlando, FL: Academic Press.
Chamberlain, Kathleen P.
    2000 *Under Sacred Ground: A History of Navajo Oil.* Albuquerque: University of New Mexico Press.
Crespi, M.
    1991 Saving Sacred Places. *National Parks* (July-August):18–19.
Cultural Survival Quarterly
    1985 Parks and People [Special Issue] 9(1) (February).
Cumming, Dorothy
    2006 *Before the Roads Were Paved: Living with the Navajos at Canyon de Chelly 1950–1952.* New Bern, NC: Trafford Publishing.
Curtis, Edward S., Horse Capture, J., Cardozo, C., and S. Momaday
    2000 *Sacred Legacy: Edward S. Curtis and the North American Indian.* New York: Simon and Schuster.
Davies, Wade
    2001 *Healing Ways: Navajo Health Care in the Twentieth Century.* Albuquerque: University of New Mexico Press.

Deloria, Vine, Jr.
  1991 *Indian Education in America*. Boulder, CO: American Indian Science and Engineering Society.
Deloria, Vine, Jr. and Clifford M. Lytle
  1984 *The Nations Within: The Past and Future of American Indian Sovereignty*. New York: Pantheon.
Doty, C. Stewart, Dale Mudge, and Herbert John Benally
  2002 *Photographing Navajos: John Collier, Jr. on the Reservation 1948–1953*. Albuquerque: University of New Mexico Press.
Dutton, Bertha
  1961 *Navajo Weaving Today*. Santa Fe: Museum of New Mexico Press.
Eachstaedt, Peter
  1994 *If You Poison Us: Uranium and Native Americans*. Santa Fe: Red Crane Books.
Evans, Lara
  1993 Bringing Together Worlds Apart. *Winds of Change: American Indian Education and Opportunity* (Boulder, CO) 8(4):1–52.
Faris, James C.
  1997 *Navajo and Photography: A Critical History of the Representation of an Indian People*. Albuquerque: University of New Mexico Press.
Federal Trade Commission
  1973 *The Trading Post System on the Navajo Reservation*. Staff report. Washington, DC: FTC.
Fletcher, S. A.
  1990 Parks, Protected Areas and Local Populations: New International Issues and Imperatives. *Landscape and Urban Planning* 19:197–201.
Goldman, Don, ed.
  1990 Interpreting Indians And Indian Cultures: A Cross-Cultural Approach. *Contact: The Southwest Region Interpreter's Newsletter* 8.
Goodman, James M.
  1982 *The Navajo Atlas: Environments, Resources, People, and History of the Diné Bikeyah*. Norman: University of Oklahoma Press.
Grant, Campbell
  1978 *Canyon de Chelly: Its People and Rock Art*. Tucson: University of Arizona Press.
Graves, Michael W.
  1994 New Directions in Americanist Archaeology. *American Antiquity* 59(1):5–8.
Griffen-Pierce, Trudy
  1992 *Earth Is My Mother, Sky Is My Father: Space, Time and Astronomy in Navajo Sand Painting*. Albuquerque: University of New Mexico Press.
Helsey, Adriel and Kenji Kawano
  2001 *In the Fifth World: Portrait of the Navajo Nation*. Tucson: Rio Nuevo
Henderson, Eric
  1989 Navajo Livestock Wealth and the Effects of Stock Reduction. *Journal of Anthropological Research* 45(4):379–404.
Hogan, Patrick
  1989 Dinétah: A Reevaluation of Pre-Revolt Navajo Occupation in Northwest New Mexico. *Journal of Anthropological Research* 45(1):53–66.
Howard, Cheryl
  1993 *Navajo Tribal Demography, 1983–1986: A Comparative and Historical Perspective*. New York: Garland.

House, Deborah
  2002 *Language Shift among the Navajos: Identity Politics and Cultural Continuity*. Tucson: University of Arizona Press.
Hunter, Wilson, and Max King
  1990 *Interpretation: "Just What Exactly Do You Do Here?"* Manuscript, Canyon de Chelly National Monument, Chinle, AZ.
Hyer, Sally
  1990 *One House, One Voice, One Heart: Native American Education at the Santa Fe Indian School*. Santa Fe: Museum of New Mexico Press.
Indian Health Service
  1990 *Navajo Area Key Statistics*. Rockville, MD: Office of Planning, Evaluation and Legislation, Division of Program Statistics.
Iverson, Peter
  1976 *The Navajos: A Critical Bibliography*. Bloomington: Indiana University Press.
  1983 *The Navajo Nation*. Albuquerque: University of New Mexico Press.
  1990 *The Navajos*. New York: Chelsea House.
Iverson, Peter and Marty Roessel
  2002 *Diné: A History of the Navajos*. Albuquerque: University of New Mexico Press.
Jett, Stephen C., with Chauncey M. Neboyia, William Morgan, Sr., and Robert W. Young
  2000 *Navajo Place Names and Trails of the Canyon de Chelly System*. New York: Peter Lang
Johnson, Broderick and Ruth Roessel, eds.
  1974 *Navajo Livestock Reduction: A National Disgrace*. Tsaile, AZ: Navajo Community College Press.
Johnson, Lupita
  1992 Living in Canyon de Chelly. *Winds of Change* (Winter):20–21.
Judd, Neil
  1968 *Men Met Along the Trail: Adventures in Archaeology*. Norman: University of Oklahoma Press.
Kelley, Klara Bonsack and Harris Francis
  1994 *Navajo Sacred Places*. Bloomington: Indiana University Press.
Kent, Kate Peck
  1985 *Navajo Weaving: Three Centuries of Change*. Santa Fe: School of American Research Press.
Kluckhohn, Clyde
  1967 *Navajo Witchcraft*. Boston: Beacon Press.
Kluckhohn, Clyde and Dorothea Leighton
  1951 *The Navaho*. Cambridge: Harvard University Press.
Kunitz, Stephen
  1983 *Disease Change and the Role of Medicine: The Navajo Experience*. Berkeley: University of California Press.
Kunitz, Stephen. J. and Jerrold E. Levy
  1991 *Navajo Aging: Transition from Family to Institutional Support*. Tucson: University of Arizona Press.
  2000 *Drinking, Conduct Disorder, and Social Change: Navajo Experiences*. Oxford: Oxford University Press
Lamphere, Louise
  1977 *To Run After Them: Cultural and Social Bases of Cooperation in a Navajo Community*. Tucson: University of Arizona Press.

1989 Historical and Regional Variability in Navajo Women's Roles. *Journal of Anthropological Research* 45(4):431–36.

Lange, F. W. and D. Leonard, eds.
1985 *Among Ancient Ruins: The Legacy of Earl Morris.* Boulder, CO: Johnson Books.

Levy, Jerrold E.
1998 *In the Beginning: The Navajo Genesis.* Berkeley: University of California Press.

Linford, Laurence D.
2000 *Navajo Places: History, Legend, Landscape.* Salt Lake City: University of Utah Press.

Lister, Florence C. and Robert H. Lister
1968 *Earl Morris and Southwestern Archaeology.* Albuquerque: University of New Mexico Press.

Locke, Raymond Friday
1990 *Sweet Salt: Navajo Folk Tales and Mythology.* Santa Monica: Round Table Publishing.

Martin, Paul and Fred Plog
1973 *The Archaeology of Arizona: A Study of the Southwest Region.* Garden City, NY: Doubleday, Natural History Press.

McCloskey, Kathy
2002 *Swept Under the Rug: A Hidden History of Navajo Weaving.* Albuquerque: University of New Mexico Press.

McCullough-Brabson, Ellen and Marilyn Help
2001 *We'll Be in Your Mountains, We'll Be In Your Songs: A Navajo Woman Sings.* Albuquerque: University of New Mexico Press.

McLuhan, T. C.
1985 *The Railroad and the American Indian 1890–1930.* New York: Harry N. Abrams.

McPherson, Robert S.
2001 *Navajo Land, Navajo Culture: The Utah Experience in the Twentieth Century.* Norman: University of Oklahoma Press.

McNitt, Frank
1962 *The Indian Traders.* Norman: University of Oklahoma Press.
1972 *Navajo Wars: Military Campaigns, Slave Raids, and Reprisals.* Albuquerque: University of New Mexico Press.

Moffett, Ben L., ed.
1981 *Canyon de Chelly Interpretive Prospectus, November 1981.* Harper's Ferry Center, VA: National Park Service.

Moore, Lucy
2004 *Into the Canyon: Seven Years in Navajo Country.* Albuquerque: University of New Mexico Press.

Morris, Ann Axtell
1934 *Digging in the Southwest.* New York: Doubleday, Duran and Co.

Morris, Don P.
1986 *Archeological Investigations at Antelope House.* Washington, DC: National Park Service.

National Park Service
1991 *Canyon Overlook: A Visitor's Guide to Canyon de Chelly National Monument.* Gallup, NM: National Park Service, Canyon de Chelly.

National Park Service, the Navajo Nation, and the Bureau of Indian Affairs
  1990 *Joint Management Plan: Canyon de Chelly National Monument*. Santa Fe: US Department of the Interior.
Navajo Nation, Technical Support Department
  1988 *Navajo Nation, Fax* [facts] 88. Window Rock, AZ: Division of Community Development.
Niethammer, Carolyn.
  2001 *I'll Go and Do More: Annie Dodge Wauneka, Navajo Leader and Activist*. Lincoln: University of Nebraska Press.
O'Neill, Colleen
  2005 *Working the Navajo Way: Labor and Culture in the Twentieth Century*. Lawrence: University Press of Kansas.
Ortiz, Alfonso, ed.
  1983 *Handbook of North American Indians, Vol. 10: Southwest*. Washington, DC: Smithsonian Institution.
Ortiz, R. D.
  1980 *American Indian Energy Resources and Development*. Albuquerque: Institute for Native American Development, University of New Mexico.
Parezo, Nancy
  1983 *Sandpainting: From Religious Act to Commercial Art*. Tucson: University of Arizona Press.
Rao, K. and C. Geisler
  1990 The Social Consequences of Protected Areas Development for Resident Populations. *Society and Natural Resources* 3:19–32.
Reichard, Gladys
  1968 *Spider Woman: A Story of Navajo Weavers and Chanters*. 1934. Reprint, Glorieta, NM: Rio Grande Press.
Reno, P.
  1981 *Mother Earth, Father Sky and Economic Development: Navajo Resources and Their Use*. Albuquerque: University of New Mexico Press.
Reyhner, Jon, Joseph Martin, Louise Lockard, and W. Sakiestewa Gilbert, eds.
  2000 *Learn in Beauty: Indigenous Education for a New Century*. Flagstaff: Northern Arizona University Center for Excellence in Education.
Rodee, Marian E.
  1995 *One Hundred Years of Navajo Rugs*. Albuquerque: University of New Mexico Press.
Roessel, Monty
  1993 *Kinaalda: A Navajo Girl Grows Up*. Minneapolis: Lerner Publications
Roessel, Ruth
  1981 *Women in Navajo Society*. Rough Rock, AZ: Navajo Resource Center.
Roessel, Ruth, ed.
  1973 *Navajo Stories of the Long Walk Period*. Tsaile, AZ: Navajo Community College Press.
Sadler, B.
  1989 National Parks, Wilderness Preservation, and Native Peoples in Northern Canada. *Natural Resources Journal* 29:185–204.
Saunders, J. M.
  1990 *Tribal and National Parks on American Indian Land*. Ph.D. dissertation, University of Arizona, Tucson.

Schaafsma, Polly
    1980 *Indian Rock Art of the Southwest*. A School of American Research book. Albuquerque: University of New Mexico Press.
Schoepfle, G. M., R. Oquita, and J. King, with I. Zohnnie, J. A. Remington, and J. K. McNeley
    1983 *Navajo Perceptions of Drinking and Drinking Behavior in The Shiprock Area*, Shiprock, New Mexico. Ethnographic report. Alcohol and Substance Abuse Project, Minority Biomedical Research Support Program, Navajo Community College, Tsaile, AZ.
Schweitzer, Marjorie M., ed.
    1999 *American Indian Grandmothers: Traditions and Transitions*. Albuquerque: University of New Mexico Press.
Schwarz, Maureen Trudelle
    2001 *Navajo Lifeways: Contemporary Issues, Ancient Knowledge*. Norman: University of Oklahoma Press.
    2003 *Blood and Voice: Navajo Women Ceremonial Practitioners*. Tucson: University of Arizona Press.
    In press *We Are Choosing Life: Navajo Perspectives on Medical and Religious Pluralism*.
Simmons, Marc
    1974 *Witchcraft in the Southwest: Spanish and Indian Supernaturalism on the Rio Grande*. Lincoln: University of Nebraska Press.
Simonelli, Jeanne
    1992 Tradition and Tourism at Canyon de Chelly. *Practicing Anthropology* 14(2):18–22.
Simonelli, Jeanne and Charles Winters
    1990 *Too Wet to Plow: The Family Farm in Transition*. New York: New Amsterdam Press.
Snead, James Elliot
    2004 *Ruins and Rivals*. Tucson: University of Arizona Press.
Spicer, Edward H.
    1962 *Cycles of Conquest: The Impact of Spain, Mexico, and the United States on the Indians of the Southwest 1533–1960*. Tucson: University of Arizona Press.
Stoker, T.
    1990 Cultural and Biological Diversity at Canyon de Chelly National Monument, Arizona. *Society and Natural Resources* 3:349–60.
Temkin-Greener, H., S. Kunitz, D. Broudy, and M. Haffner
    1981 Surgical Fertility Regulation among Women on The Navajo Indian Reservation 1972–1978. *American Journal of Public Health* 71(4).
Thompson, Gerald
    1976 *The Army and The Navajo: The Bosque Redondo Reservation Experiment 1863–1868*. Tucson: University of Arizona Press.
Towner, Ronald H., ed.
    1996 *The Archaeology of Navajo Origins*. Salt Lake City: University of Utah Press.
Trahant, LeNora Begay
    1996 *The Success of the Navajo Arts and Crafts Enterprise: A Retail Success Story*. New York: Walker and Company
Travis, Scott
    2005 *Cooperative Watershed Restoration Project: Tamarisk and Russian Olive Management at Canyon de Chelly National Monument. Final Environmental Assessment*.

Canyon de Chelly National Monument, Arizona: National Park Service, U.S. Department of the Interior.

Trimble, Stephen
1993 *The People: Indians of the American Southwest.* Santa Fe: School of American Research Press.

Underhill, Ruth
1956 *The Navajos.* Norman: University of Oklahoma Press.

Weber, Sandra S.
1990 Interpreting Our "Cultural Ecosystem." *CRM Bulletin* 13(3).

West, Patrick C.
1991 *Resident Peoples and National Parks.* Tucson: University of Arizona Press.

Winds of Change: American Indian Education and Opportunity
n.d. *Quarterly Journal of the American Indian Science and Engineering Society.* Various issues. Boulder, CO: AISES.

Yazzie, Ethelou
1971 *Navajo History.* Rough Rock, AZ: Navajo Curriculum Center, Rough Rock Demonstration School.

Zolbrod, Paul G.
1984 *Diné Bahane: The Navajo Creation Story.* Albuquerque: University of New Mexico Press.

Zolbrod, Paul and Roseann S. Willink.
1996 *Weaving a World: Textiles and the Navajo Way of Seeing.* Santa Fe: Museum of New Mexico Press

Zube, E. H. and M. L. Busch
1990 Park-People Relationships: An International Review. *Landscape and Urban Planning* 19:117–31.